# *When A Rose*

# *Is Not A*

# *Rose*

by Rebecca D. Larson

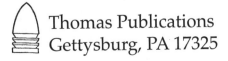
Thomas Publications
Gettysburg, PA 17325

ISBN-1-57747-053-2

Cover design by Ryan C. Stouch

*To* my husband, my daughter, and my mother who tolerate all of my research projects and encourage me in all of my undertakings.

"During all periods of the war, instances occurred of women being found in the ranks, fighting as common soldiers, their sex remaining unsuspected, and the particular motive in each case often unknown."

—Frank Moore, 1866

# CONENTS

## *A Woman In The Ranks?*

I came across your story,
    One late afternoon;
The story that haunted me,
    I read it in June.

The clipping was short,
    It said you had died;
And when they opened the grave,
    Eight lay by your side.

Who were you I wonder,
    Brave soldier in blue;
What possesses a woman
    To do what you'd do?

From whence comes the bravery,
    The stamina, the call?
To fight with the men
    To give it your all.

What overcomes a woman
    To drop her skirts so long,
Take up a cause to fight;
    Whether right or wrong?

Did anyone grieve,
    Or hold tight your hand?
As your blood did flow freely,
    Soaking the land?

To Shiloh you went
    And at Shiloh you died,
They opened the grave
    Eight lay by your side.

For seventy-two years,
    You lay there unknown,
For seventy-two years
    You were not alone.

Did your comrades know
    As a woman you lied
Yet as they knew as a man
    You had died?

You now lay in honor,
    Your life blood all spent,
You fought for the Union,
    Yes to Shiloh you went.

And when they all argue,
    Should woman fight,
I know you must smile,
    Somewhere in the night.

What a question of folly,
    To stir mild strife,
For a woman who lay down
    And gave up her life.

For when the grave was opened
    It could not be denied,
A soldier, a woman,
    And eight lay by your side.

Oh what was your name,
    My sister in blue,
What possesses a woman,
    To do what you'd do?

If only I could reach back,
    Past the long ago years,
Hold tight your hand,
    And give you my tears.

—Tara Harl-Odom

# INTRODUCTION

Civil War historians estimate more than four hundred women disguised as men fought in the War Between the States. With appropriate attire, women could easily deceive others as to their gender. Secrecy was their key to success. So successful were they that little is known about these heroines. Most were discovered only when wounded or killed. Some revealed their gender when their husbands or lovers were discharged and they chose to be dismissed with them. Some of the ladies wrote letters home while others died without their true identities being revealed.

Most believed so deeply in the Cause that their gender did not deter them from the battlefield. Some saw themselves as Joan of Arc, as the press praised those ladies who rushed to enlistment offices in an effort to serve their country. As late as June 7, 1864, the *New York Herald* was lauding the lady soldiers as "spunky and plucky."

Many, however, looked on the ladies as mentally deranged or immoral. Mrs. Mary Livermore, writing in her book, *My Story Of The War*, believed female soldiers' "service was not the noblest that women rendered during the war."

The official records of General Pickett's Division tell of a husband and wife team being killed in Pickett Charge's at Gettysburg. One private in the 14th Iowa was discovered to be a girl. So upset was the young woman at being discovered that she committed suicide.[1]

Many women went to the battlefield legally and without disguise as vivandieres. The responsibilities of the vivandiere were to bring water and munitions to the soldiers during the battle as well as cook, wash, nurse, and operate the regimental sutler shop selling luxuries not issued by the government.

Some women tried to organize entire regiments of soldiers. Sallie Reneau of Mississippi petitioned Governor Pettus to allow her to raise a regiment of armed uniformed female soldiers to be called the "Mississippi Nightingales." Her petition was denied.

Women tried to serve in many ways—as individual soldiers, as part of an organized group, with husbands and without. Some were discovered easily and returned home. Others, perhaps by ingenuity or even sheer luck, escaped discovery and served for long periods of time, until by choice or by wounding they left the field of battle and went home. Still others served until death, and were buried with their comrades in arms who never knew they had been fighting side by side with someone's mother, sister, wife, or daughter.

# THE ORGANIZATIONS

## NANCY HARTS

The Nancy Harts were organized in 1861, to train young ladies to become sharpshooters. This group of Confederate women was named after Nancy Hart, a Georgia Revolutionary War heroine who captured six British officers and soldiers, then shot two soldiers who did not believe she would pull the trigger.

Under the direction of Mrs. J. Brown Morgan, the wife of a major in the 6th Georgia Infantry, and Mrs. Peter Heard, a local minister's wife, the Nancy Harts were credited with saving La Grange, Georgia from being looted and pillaged by Northern marauders. The ladies wore ruffled skirts with flower trimmed hats as they defended their homes and their neighbors' property.

On April 17, 1865, the Nancy Harts' only official battle occurred against a detachment of Wilson's Raiders. The Confederate ladies met the Yankee soldiers in the town square with guns drawn. The ladies, ordered to surrender, agreed to do so only after the Yankees agreed to go through the town without burning any property or taking anything. La Grange was left unscathed unlike many Southern cities due to the tenacity of the Nancy Harts.

## RHEA COUNTY GIRLS

In Rhea County, Tennessee, a group of women organized a cavalry company much like the Nancy Harts. It is easy to understand why this group was organized. Most of the ladies were in the sixteen to eighteen year old bracket, with no one over the age of twenty-one. Barbara Allen's father was in a Union prison and she had three brothers with General Lee and one with General J. E. Johnston. Robby Thomison had three brothers; one was wounded at Shiloh, and another brother at Chickamauga, and the third one marched with General Lee. The girls were all deeply involved in the war through their families.

They wore traditional clothing during the day as most were from prominent Southern families. When the sun set, the "girls" dressed in their uniforms of trousers with a short skirt over the top much like the vivandieres. They set up picket lines, scouted enemy batteries, and drilled so they were all expert marksmen and riders. They never saw action but they served the Confederate army in a reconnaissance capacity.

The Rhea County Girls were trained by three cavalry captains. The first group was organized by Captain W. T. Glass in August 1861. The second was amassed by Captain Bert Lenty in April 1862. The third was under the direction of Captain W. T. Darwin and began in May 1862. On most occasions, the three units acted in tandem, as they performed their duties.

The Union Army considered the Rhea County girls a real threat. They were a mounted unit with most riding on plantation saddles, but a few did have McClellan saddlery. They acted successfully until 1865.

Captain John P. Walker organized a Union unit called the Goon's Hog Back Regulars for the sole purpose of destroying the ladies' rebellion. All sixteen ladies were rounded up like cattle and marched to Bell's Landing fifteen miles away. Herded onto a barge called the *Chicken Thief*, they were transported to Chattanooga, Tennessee, to be tried before General Steadman.

When they appeared before Steadman, their captor was severely reprimanded by his commanding officer. Steadman paroled the Rhea County Girls after they were forced to take an oath of allegiance to the United States. He had them escorted to the Planter's Hotel where they were served the best meal Steadman could arrange. Walker was ordered to return the ladies to Bell's Landing. Infuriated because the girls had not been punished, he left them to their own devices to secure transport back to Rhea County. As the girls journeyed home, they were grieved to learn of Lee's surrender at Appomatox.

The complete roster of the Rhea County Girls is as follows:

> Mary McDonald, Commander
> Caroline McDonald, First Lieutenant
> Ann Payne, Second Lieutenant
> Rhodie Thomison, Third Lieutenant
> Jane Keith, First Sergeant
> Rachel Howell, Second Sergeant
> Sallie Mitchell, Third Sergeant
> Minerva Tucker, Fourth Sergeant

| | | |
|---|---|---|
| Mary Paine | Mary Keith | Martha Bell |
| Margaret Keith | Mary Crawford | Jane Paine |
| Sidney McDonald | Jennie Hoyal | Anne Meyers |
| Martha Early | Mary Robertson | Sarah Rudd |
| Josephine Allen | Mary Ann McDonald | Sarah Hoyal |
| Kate Dunwoody | Ann Gillespie | Jane Locke |
| Barbara Allen | Margaret Sykes | Kate Hoyal |

The *Dayton Herald* reported the death of Mary McDonald Sawyers, former captain of the Rhea County Girls, on December 18, 1915. Mary died on December 14, in Hixon, Hamilton County, Tennessee, at the age of seventy-three. Services were held at the Southern Methodist Church of Dayton by Rev. James Burnett. Mary had asked that no flowers be sent to her funeral and that all contributions be sent to the Southern orphans' homes. The full military services at her graveside were conducted by the J. W. Gillespie Camp Number 923.

## BESS DELL AND COMPANY

Bess Dell and Company was formed of mothers and daughters in the Athens, Georgia, area. The ladies served as a home guard to protect their neighborhood "rights, liberty, and honor." The group trained using William J. Hardee's *Rifle And Light Infantry Tactics* handbook, and met twice each week to march and drill. Bess Dell and Company became expert marksmen with their available weapons. The lady soldiers were attired in uniforms of red calico bound with blue. A proud resident wrote to her sister in Tennessee, "You know how nervous and timid Millie was. Well now she can load a gun and fire and hit a spot a good distance. Millie belongs to Bess Dell and Company, you know."

## FAUQUIER COUNTY, VIRGINIA, WOMEN

The Fauquier County, Virginia, women formed a militia of sorts to help General John Mosby escape the Federal movements. The women's activities were recorded in the Black Horse Cavalry memoirs. The ladies stood picket guard while Mosby's Raiders slept, fed, and housed both men and horses, and supplied information on Federal activities, often walking or riding miles to warn of advancing troops. Their activities must have been successful, for the Federal Secret Service sent a woman detective in the summer of 1863 to infiltrate their unit. Ann Waters, as she was called, gathered enough information to have several of the women arrested.

## THE UNKNOWNS

Female soldiers were recorded in diaries and letters sent home. Sergeant Rufus Mead of the 5th Connecticut Volunteers wrote in his diary of the arrest of two unidentified female soldiers. One Missouri soldier wrote home in February 1863:

> ...We discovered last week a soldier who turned out to be
> a girl. She had already been in service for twenty-one months

and was twice wounded. Maybe she would have remained undiscovered for a long time if she hadn't fainted. She was given a warm bath which gave the secret away.[2]

Provost Marshal General Marsena R. Patrick's diary entry of August 26, 1862, tells of a flag of truce being raised to exchange a prisoner who belonged to General Franz Sigel's unit who was, "...a woman in man's dress."[3]

Susan B. Anthony reported two female soldiers serving in the 59th Ohio Regiment. The ladies served three years.[4]

Dr. J. R. Edicon of the 148th Illinois recorded the death of a female soldier at the United States General Hospital in Tullahoma, Tennessee, in April 1865.

In 1934, Shiloh National Military Park unearthed the remains of nine fallen Federal soldiers. One was a female with a minie ball buried in her chest.

The New Albany, Indiana, *Ledger* reported that the 66th Indiana had a female volunteer in Captain Gerard's company. She was a resident of Six-Mile Switch on the Louisville and Chicago Railroad system. She was never suspected of being a female, although she had been in camp for four weeks. Her uncle visited Camp Noble and recognized her. She cried when her gender was revealed. Commander Martin discharged her and sent her home. As she was from an affluent family, her name was suppressed.[5]

The only surviving sibling of a family of four children traveled to Windsor, Ohio, cut her hair, and dressed in boy's clothes. Then she went to Detroit to be a "substitute" for an enrolled man. She went to four recruiters who rejected her because she was too short. The fifth recruiter stripped "the boy" and he rushed from the room in astonishment. The young woman was reprimanded (once she replaced her clothing). She remained determined to enlist and avenge the deaths of her three brothers.[6]

One female recruit made headlines in the Maysville, Kentucky, *Dollar Weekly Bulletin* on November 27, 1862. "The sex of the female recruit in Rochester was discovered by her trying to put her pants on over her head."[7]

Two women involved in the Battle of Lookout Mountain served under Generals Bragg and Blair. One died at the battle site while the second was mustered out with her regiment.[8]

# THE WOMEN

## ARABELLA GRIFFITH BARLOW

Arabella Griffith Barlow, a native of New Jersey, enlisted in the 61st New York Infantry with her husband, Francis C. Barlow, a young Harvard Law School graduate. Francis had enlisted in the military the day before their wedding. The duo left for Washington on April 21 where they camped out for four months. They were stationed at Harpers Ferry under the command of General Patterson. The regiment was mustered out in September 1861.

Francis and Arabella reenlisted in November 1861, with Francis being promoted to lieutenant colonel of the 61st New York Infantry. He became known as the "boy general" because of his young age. They wintered in camp at Alexandria, Virginia.

The 61st, under the command of Gen. George B. McClellan, participated in the Virginia Peninsula Campaign in 1862. The campaign was a failure and the regiment moved north just in time for the Maryland Campaign.

Colonel Barlow was wounded on September 17, 1862. Arabella cared for him, nursing him back to health. The Colonel was promoted to brigadier general while convalescing and given command of the 11th Corps at Chancellorsville and Gettysburg.

General Barlow was wounded at Gettysburg and taken prisoner by Confederate General John B. Gordon. Arabella took matters into her own hands to rescue her husband and appealed directly to Gordon. Gordon took compassion on the young couple and released Barlow primarily because he believed him to be dying from his wounds.

General Barlow and Arabella returned to the heat of battle in April 1864 with Francis taking command of a division of the 2nd Corps. He led the troops into the Battle of Petersburg. Arabella cared for the wounded and rallied the retreating soldiers, as she had done in the past.

Her long days and nights on the battlefield soon took its toll as typhoid fever struck her fatigued body. Arabella died on July 27, 1864, in Washington. She was praised for her support of the soldiers.

After the war, Gen. Barlow resumed his law practice, and founded the American Bar Association. He joined his precious Arabella on January 11, 1896.

## MARY AND MOLLY BELL

Mary and Molly Bell enlisted in the Confederate Army as Tom Parker and Bob Martin, respectively. They served two years under General Jubal Early. A captain had them arrested when their sex was revealed, claiming that they demoralized the troops. The young women were imprisoned at Castle Thunder. The dates of their imprisonment are incomplete so historians can not ascertain whether the Bell sisters were incarcerated when Mollie Bean was. The *Richmond Examiner* reported the girls were sent home, still wearing their uniforms, and "perfectly disconsolate at being separated from their male counterparts." That paper also stated on October 31, 1864, that [the sisters were imprisoned for] "aiding in the demoralization of General Early's veterans. The sisters were busy with activities other than sniping."

## ELIZABETH MALINDA PRITCHARD BLAYLOCK

Elizabeth Malinda Pritchard, daughter of Alfred and Elizabeth Gregg Pritchard married William McKesson Blaylock in 1856. Blaylock, a Union supporter, refused to enlist in the Confederate military in 1861, but later recanted and joined Company F of the 26th North Carolina Infantry in March 1862. Malinda cut her hair and enlisted as Sam Blaylock, William's younger brother. Sam, at five feet four inches in height, weighing one hundred thirty pounds, performed the duties of a veteran soldier.

William planned to desert at the earliest opportunity. Deciding a medical discharge was more satisfactory than being labeled a deserter, William rubbed poison sumac berries over his skin. The medical personnel judged Blaylock unfit for service and discharged him on April 20, 1862. Sam, in order to join William, was forced to disrobe to the waist to prove her femininity claim. A surprised commander released Sam the same day as William.

After their release, the Blaylocks returned home to Grandfather Mountain, North Carolina. When William's skin disease disappeared, his Confederate neighbors nagged him for not returning to duty. To escape harassment, the Blaylocks moved to the East Tennessee wilderness but they were pursued by the anxious neighbors and William was wounded by gunfire. The pair also assisted Yankee prisoners escaping into Tennessee. During one of these escapades, Malinda was wounded in the shoulder and William had one of his eyes shot out.

After the war, the Blaylocks lived out their lives in Avery County, Tennessee. Malinda died in 1903, and William in 1913, at the age of seventy-seven. His death was the result of a railroad accident.

According to National Archives records dated April 20, 1862, of Company F, 26th North Carolina Volunteers, a young woman enlisted in 1862. She donned the Confederate gray, collected a fifty dollar bounty, and drilled with other men as a veteran soldier. She fought in several battles before her sex was revealed. To avoid arrest, the young woman, named Mrs. S. M. Blaylock, returned both the bounty and the uniform and returned home.

*Elizabeth "Sam" Blaylock holding a photo of her husband.*
(Southern Historical Collection, University of North Carolina, Chapel Hill)

# KADY McKENSIE BROWNELL

Kady McKensie was born in Caffaria, South Africa, in December 1842, to Angus McKensie, a Scottish soldier serving in the British army. Kady's mother, Alice, was the unit's color bearer. In 1861, Kady married Robert Brownell in Providence, Rhode Island. Robert enlisted as an orderly in the 1st and later the 5th Rhode Island Infantry. The unit was a company of sharpshooters.

It was only natural for Kady to accompany Robert. Like her mother, she became a color bearer rolling her heavy standard in a leather case and marching alongside the troopers. Kady, stocky and strong, carried her standard from Washington into battle. The colors were unfurled just prior to gunfire. She trained daily with the men asking no favors or special privileges.

Kady carried the colors into the First Battle of Bull Run. She saved many lives by placing herself in a position to rally the men. Her husband marched with Company H when the regiment advanced. Kady's standard was visible, rallying the sharpshooters. Kady and her colors were in the center of a long line as the troops moved into battle. Her black hair was wet with perspiration and powered with dust as she marched on, into the heat of the conflict, urging the men ever forward. Kady was the focus of attacks, but she never faltered and stood her ground, bearing her colors bravely.

The line gave and troops retreated toward Kady. A few men stood with her. Confederate cannonballs fell like hail around her—but she continued to bear her colors defiantly. One of the soldiers saw her, grabbed her by the arm, and dragged her out of danger's way, shouting, "Come, sis, there's no use to stay here to be killed—let's get into the woods." Her rescuer was shot as they ran toward the trees, and he fell dead at her feet. Kady had to leave him there and keep running to stay alive. The Rebels were advancing; the fatigued Kady, having been on the battlefield for six hours, found an ambulance with just enough room for her. Bullets from the Rebel troops flew around the ambulance, and a minie ball ripped through the canvas cover. Kady retreated from the transport and, finding a saddled horse, she mounted and quickly rode to Centerville where she was safe for awhile.

Kady's thoughts turned toward her spouse's safety. Her horse was confiscated by an officer before she reached her destination in search of her husband, so Kady walked the remainder of the way. When she reached Alexandria, the city was in chaos. It took a while for Kady to locate General Burnside but finally she learned her husband was safe. Burnside gave Kady a horse to ride to her husband's unit.

*Kady Brownwell.*

Once the couple was reunited, Kady resumed carrying the colors. She carried her standard into the Battles of Fairfax Court House, Roanoke Island, and the Second Bull Run. Kady was wounded at the Battle of New Bern. Though she was injured, Kady took the risk of helping a fallen Confederate officer out of a muddy creek bottom, and was rewarded with a curse. Her first impulse was to impale the officer on a nearby bayonet, but she resisted.

Her husband received a serious leg wound during the Battle of New Bern. Kady was allowed to nurse him. When Robert Brownell was medically discharged in September 1863, Kady ended her tour of duty, also.

Clinton Scollard wrote a poem honoring Kady:

> "While the mad rout of Manassas was surging,
> When those around her fled wildly, or fell,
> And the bold Beauregard onward urging,
> Who so undaunted as Kady Brownell."

## FLORENA BUDWIN

Florena Budwin joined the Union forces to be with her husband, a Pennsylvania artillery captain. She maintained her disguise throughout her military career. The husband and wife were captured by the Confederates and incarcerated in Andersonville Prison, where Captain Budwin died. Florence was transferred to the prison in Florence, South Carolina, when Federals threatened to overrun the area. She grew seriously ill and the physicians discovered her sex. Although she was given special care, it was too little, too late, and Florence died on January 25, 1865. She was buried in Florence, South Carolina, National Cemetery.

## CAPTAIN BILLY

Bartlett S. Johnston wrote letters home describing an officer in charge of escorting Yankee prisoners from the Battle of Chickamauga. Johnston was, at the time:

> ...standing on a Baltimore platform [while] one company of the troops got off of the train and formed a line. The officer in command (a captain) was a woman dressed in full uniform with a tobacco bag tied on a button of her coat...the men called her "Captain Billy." They told me her husband had been the captain and she a lieutenant but that he was killed and she made captain and put in command of the company and that she had been wounded. I ran over to where General D. H. Hill was standing and called his attention to the fact that a woman was over here in command of a company. He told me: "My boy, that woman is an example for some of these men staying at home. I would like to know what regiment she belongs to.

## AMY CLARKE

Amy Clarke, also known as Richard Anderson, was born in Iuka, Tennessee. She joined the Louisiana Cavalry for seven months before she was able to join her husband, Walter, in the 11th Tennessee according to an account published in the *Jackson Mississippian* on December 30, 1862. She and Walter served under General Braxton Bragg.

Walter was killed at Shiloh on April 6, 1862. The *Jackson Mississippian* reported that Amy personally buried Walter on that battlefield. She continued fighting in the ranks, and was twice wounded: once in the ankle, and once in the breast.

The *Cairo City Gazette,* dated December 25, 1862, reported Amy's capture by the Yankees. During her incarceration as a prisoner of war, her gender was revealed. Amy was released to Confederate officers, clothed in female attire. A week after her release, she was seen in Jackson, Mississippi, making her way back to General Bragg's troops. No information is recorded of her later life.

## FRANCES LOUISA CLAYTON

Frances Louisa Clayton was determined to accompany her husband into battle when he enlisted in a Minnesota regiment. Mr. Clayton procured a uniform and mustache for Frances. While serving under General William S. Rosencrans in Tennessee, during the Battle of Stone's River, Private Clayton was killed just five steps away from his spouse.

According to *Frank Leslie's llustrated Newspapers,* "She charged over his body with the rear line, driving the Rebels with the bayonet but was soon struck with a ball in the hip, and conveyed to the hospital, where her sex was, of course, discovered." Another copy of *Frank Leslie's Illustrated Newspapers* continued Frances' story. "While in the army, the better to conceal her sex, she [Frances] learned to drink, smoke, chew, and swear with the best, or worst of the soldiers. She stood guard, went on picket duty, in rain, and storm, and fought on the field with the rest and was considered a good fighting man."

After the war, while being transferred between Nashville and Louisville, the train she was riding on was attached by marauders. They relieved the tall, tanned, masculine woman of her currency and her valuables. Where Frances traveled after the robbery is unknown.

## LIZZIE COOK

Lizzie Cook of Aponoose County, Iowa, joined the 5th Kansas as William Ross. Her father was killed at Walnut Creek, Linn County, Missouri, while serving in the 1st Missouri State Militia. Her brother was a sergeant in the 5th Kansas Infantry. Lizzie went to Keokuk and worked until she earned enough to buy a suit of boy's clothes.

Her disguise lasted for a brief time as her polite manner gave away her gender. After her discharge, Lizzie joined the Union Aid Society but was greatly disappointed with the organization as it was more of a social group than an soldier's aid organization.

## MARY CORBIN

Mary Corbin was a Unionist from Hillsboro, Tennessee, who was driven away by her father, a Southern sympathizer. She joined Sergeant John Wesley Marshall, of Wagner's Brigade, Woods' Division,

*The Battle of Chickamauga.* (Library of Congress)

who had proposed to her on an earlier occasion. Mary was captured by Colonel Cobb Corbin of the Army of the Cumberland when Woods' Division retreated from the Chickamauga Campaign along the Tennessee River. She was accused of being a spy.

When Mary told her sad story, Corbin was sympathetic and sent her to Chattanooga escorted by a chaplain. Mary remained in Chattanooga until she had the opportunity to reenlist a short time later.

## MRS. CURTIS

Mrs. Curtis of a Rochester, New York regiment was captured by Confederates and sent to Richmond. The *Richmond Whig* reported, "She was young but, by no means prepossessing." (Some historical reports show Mrs. Curtis as Mrs. Custis.)

Mrs. Curtis wore velvet chevrons on the sleeves of her garment. A small hat adorned with a bugle-shaped brass ornament was cocked on one side of her saucy head. When she was captured, Mrs. Curtis gave her accostors a verbal thrashing. She showed no fear as the Confederates escorted her to the quarters where she would be confined.

Mrs. Curtis could not be sent to the Confederate military prisons as ladies were not incarcerated in such facilities. The captors rented a private residence for her. After her release, she disappeared into the pages of history.

# BRIDGET DIVERS

Bridget Divers, often reported as Deavers or Devens, joined the 1st Michigan Cavalry as a vivandiere so she could be with her husband. Bridget rode a government horse and carried weapons to soldiers who had lost or damaged theirs during battle. She stood guard duty day or night, rode on raids against the Confederates and assumed command when officers fell. Bridget had three horses shot out from under her in battle and lost ten during the war.

The soldiers described Bridget as a rough and tumble character, kind-hearted, vigorous, and common, a stout, leather-faced woman with a cheery disposition. She was fearless and daring, often taking the place of fallen soldiers fighting heroically. She never allowed troops to retreat. On at least two occasions, Bridget brought retreating troopers back to the battlefront and prevented a defeat.

Near Dinwiddie, during a heavy skirmish, the commander was killed. Bridget rode into the heat of the battle amid Confederate and Union bayonets and placed the dead captain on her horse. The following tale comes from the writings of Mrs. M. M. Husband:

> Biddy (as Bridget was often called) rode with the men during Sheridan's raids. During one particular cavalry battle, the captain was killed and the colonel was wounded. Biddy personally oversaw the movement of the colonel by train to the field hospital at City Point—working for ninety-six hours without rest. Only when the colonel was safely lodged in the hospital, did Biddy rest for twentyfour hours as she traveled back to the front. Back under fire, Biddy discovered the captain's corpse had not been removed the battlefield because it was too dangerous. Biddy with the assistance of an orderly, rode into the hail of minie balls, heaved the body on her horse and then rode seven miles to an undertaker to have the body embalmed. After the body was prepared, Biddy again strapped it to her horse and rode to a coffin maker. After the coffin was finished, Biddy forwarded the body on to the captain's family in Michigan.
>
> When Biddy returned to the battlefront, the third time, there were still wounded suffering in the field. She complained to the generals—they ignored her. "Furnish me some ambulances and I will bring them in." She was given four wagons with teams and drivers. In a matter of hours, ten wounded men were being transported to a field hospital. Only a few miles from the hospital, the caravan was stopped by Southern soldiers who in spite of Biddy's pleas, took the horses, mules, and other articles they deemed of importance as the drivers fled.

A heartbroken Biddy was jubilant when a Union officer rode by, surveyed the situation and secured horses and drivers for the conveyances. The wounded were soon being treated at City Point Hospital and Biddy returned to the battlefront on a fresh mount.

During the Battle of Fair Oaks/Seven Pines, Bridget rallied the retreating Union regiment and put the troops back in action. Bridget urged the men on, "Go in, boys, and bate the bloody spalpeens, and revenge me husband." Her words brought the Union soldiers back to the battlefront, probably fearing the wrath of Bridget more than the Confederate gunfire.

Mrs. Charlotte E. McKay, a Civil War nurse who kept a detailed diary, wrote on March 28, 1865:

> Visiting, in company with miss Bridget Deavers, two large camps of dismounted cavalrymen lying along the James River...Bridget or as the men called her, Biddy—has probably seen more of the hardship and danger than any other woman during the War. She has been with the cavalry all of the time, going out with them on their cavalry raids—always ready to succor the wounded on the field-often getting men off who, but for her, would be left to die, and fearless of shell or bullet, among the last to leave.
>
> Protected by officers and respected by privates, with her little sunburnt face, she makes her home in the saddle or the shelter-tent, often, indeed, sleeping in the open air without a tent, and by her courage and devotion "winning golden opinions from all sorts of people." She is an Irish woman, has been in the country sixteen years, and is now twenty-six years of age.

Frank Moore recorded Bridget's activities in *Women Of The War: Their Heroism And Self Sacrifice*, writing that,

> ...when the brigade was in active service, she was with it in the field, and shared all its dangers. She was a fearless and skillful rider, and as brave as the bravest under fire...sleeping on the ground like a soldier and enduring hardships like the rest, her face has become browned by exposure, and her figure grown athletic by constant exercise and life in the open air. But the heart that beats under her plaid cassock is as full of womanly tenderness as that of any princess in purple velvet. She sometimes went out with the men on picket and remained all night on watch. At times, when sickness or hard service had thinned the ranks of the regiment, she would take the place of a soldier, and go out...doing the full duty of a soldier.

By the time the Michigan regiment was mustered out on March 10, 1866, Bridget had become so accustomed to military life that civilian life was a bore. Bridget tried to be a homemaker for a brief time, but soon enlisted in a regular army cavalry unit stationed in the western United States territories. The last record of Bridget was in the late 1870s when she served in the Indian Wars. Where she expired or how is unknown. The heroic "Irish Biddy" has no tombstone marking her final resting place.

## DUTCH MARY

John Haley, while serving in the 17th Maine Infantry, wrote in his journal on December 1862, that a vivandiere called Dutch Mary worked within the ranks. He recorded her contributions by writing:

> ...she cooks and washes for the officers, thereby earning an honest penny. when the battle rages, she is on hand to minister to the needs of the wounded. When in camp, she sometimes drills with the men, as today, and she can go through it as well as any. The way her legs fly when executing a wheeling operation reminds me of some swift moving insect...with her tight Zouave suit on, she looks like a man. One private thinking to have some sport at her expense, came up behind her as she was washing some clothes at the brook and kissed her. She seized a wet shirt and belabored him right and left, pursuing him out of camp, to the great amusement of his comrades, and chagrin of himself. When next he felt in a jocose frame of mind, no doubt he didn't take Dutch Mary as the object of his mirth.

## SARAH EMMA EVELYN EDMONDS

Sarah Emma Evelyn Edmonds was born in December 1841, in Canada. She fled to the United States when her father arranged her marriage to a neighbor twice her age in exchange for a small herd of cattle. Sarah cut her hair, stole a set of boy's clothes from a neighbor's clothesline, and assumed the persona of Franklin Thompson to escape her father.

She traveled to Hartford, Connecticut, sustaining herself by doing chores and odd jobs for meals and lodging along the way. Once in Hartford, Sarah secured a position as a Bible salesman. During her journeys through Michigan selling Bibles, Sarah met William R. Morse, a fellow peddler. The two became fast friends, even though Morse did not know Thompson was a female.

When the War Between the States began, the two friends made an attempt to enlist in the Union army. William was accepted but Franklin (Sarah) was rejected because she was too short. She was finally mustered into Company F, 2nd Michigan Cavalry on May 14, 1861, as a male nurse.

Franklin served as a military nurse for a brief time before General George McClellan asked Franklin to perform several feats of espionage. Franklin volunteered for spy duty when a close friend (who did not know Franklin was Sarah) was killed during the Peninsula Campaign. Franklin undertook eleven spying expeditions in all, and used disguises such as an Irish peddler woman, a Confederate youth, a grieving widow, and an emancipated slave named Ned. For the latter role, it was necessary for Franklin to stain her hands and face with black walnut hulls sealed by silver nitrate she procured from the hospital, which gave her skin a gray black color. The color lasted about two months.

One Mrs. Butler, the wife of an Army chaplain in Franklin's unit, was the only person who knew Sarah's true identity. She helped her with her costumes for the spy missions.

Franklin fought at the battles of Blackburn's Ford, Williamsburg, Fair Oaks, Richmond, Antietam, and Fredericksburg. Franklin buried a fellow female soldier at Antietam.

*Sarah Emma Edmonds*
*as Franklin Thompson.*
(State Archives of Michigan)

Comrades respected Franklin as a tough, energetic young man who was a skillful horseman and an excellent marksman. Daman Stewart never knew his bunkmate was a woman. He wrote in his diary, "men teased Franklin about his small boots and called him 'our little woman' since he was smaller and more delicately built than others...said in fun and no one questioned Frank seriously. He showed good common sense."

Franklin became ill from malaria in 1863, and deserted on April 22 before her secret could be revealed. Sarah assumed her female identity and served as a battlefield nurse after her recuperation. She continued to serve in that capacity until war's end.

After the war, Sarah married Linus H. Seelye and moved to LaPorte, Texas. On a whim, Sarah attended the 1884 regimental reunion. Her fellow soldiers questioned her and were satisfied that she was Franklin. The men encouraged Sarah to apply for a monthly pension.

Congress initially wanted to try Sarah as a deserter. Her fellow soldiers began to testify on her behalf. House of Representatives member, E. B. Winans of Michigan, introduced House Bill 5335, which sought to exonerate Sarah. "Though by the rules of war, a deserter, yet...her course and conduct after the war shows the same zeal in the service of her country in her proper character as activated by her when she first dedicated herself to the cause which she felt to be the highest and noblest that can actuate man or woman."

Many members of the Michigan units came to Sarah's rescue telling of her exploits. William Shakespeare of Company K and Albert E. Cowles of Lansing, who were in charge of supplies for the brigade hospital, worked with Franklin daily and had "no ideas Frank was a she." Colonel Frederick Schneider is quoted as saying, "Frank was dependable and conscientious. I had no idea Frank was a woman." Testimonies from Generals Irving McDowell, Daniel Tyler, and Samuel P. Heintzelman verified her activities during the Battles of Bull Run and Centerville. William Boston of Company H, 29th Michigan Volunteers Infantry wrote in his diary of Franklin, "We are having quite a time at the expense of our brigadier postmaster. He turns out to be a girl and has deserted. She went by the name of Frank Thompson and was a pretty girl. She came out with Company F of the Second Michigan Regiment and has been with them ever since."

General John Robertson wrote in his book entitled *Michigan In The War*, published in 1882:

> In Company F, Second Michigan Infantry, there enlisted at Flint, Franklin (or Frank as [he was] usually called), aged twenty, ascertained afterwards and about the time he left the regiment to have been a female, and a good-looking one at

that. She succeeded in concealing her sex most admirably, serving in various campaigns and battles of the regiment as a soldier; [she was] often employed as a spy, going within the enemy's lines, sometimes absent for weeks, and is said to have furnished much valuable information.

She remained with the regiment until April 1863, when it is supposed she apprehended a disclosure of her sex and deserted at Lebanon, Kentucky, but where she went remains a mystery.

General Oliver O. Howard was shot in the arm during a skirmish. Franklin sprang from her mount to nurse him. When she returned to her horse for bandages and dressings, the animal spooked, wheeled, and kicked Franklin, injuring her almost as bad as Howard. She could not seek medical attention until she was safely back at the camp where Mrs. Butler could care for her. Howard told the story to Franklin's desertion hearing before Congress.

Several other fellow soldiers asked to testify on Franklin's behalf. They were Richard Holstead, James Reid, Sam Houlton, and Robert Bostwick. Judge Albert E. Cowles of Lansing, Michigan, served with the 20th Michigan Infantry while Franklin was at brigade headquarters, and he, too, testified for her.

Captain William R. Morse could not believe that Sarah Seelye was Franklin Thompson so he arranged a visit with her. He later testified before the Congressional hearings: "In a few minutes the lady made her appearance and recognized me. I spent a very pleasant hour in talking over old times and listening to the story of her life...I do know that S. Emma Seelye is the identical Franklin Thompson." One reporter, after the interview, quoted Sarah as saying:

> It is true that my discharge from the service did not come the "red tape" line but by a more direct route—simply that of leaving on my own account...but from my standpoint I never for a moment considered myself a deserter. I simply left because I could hold out no longer, and to remain and become a helpless patient in a hospital was sure discovery which to me was far worse than death.

A report was sent by officers and privates of the late 2nd Regiment of Michigan Infantry and read before the House of Representatives. "In view of her many ministrations of tenderness and mercy, thousand of soldiers who were the recipients of her timely attention and nursing must remember her with the most filial regard. She is now the same true, loyal woman that she was in those eventful stormy days of 1861 to 1865, when the country was passing [through] the agonizing throes of civil war." Congressman Byron M. Cutcheon of Michigan's Ninth

District, a former colonel of the 20th Michigan Infantry, pursued the passage of the bill to free Sarah of desertion charges and grant her pension.

Sarah and Linus were living in LaPorte, Texas, when Sarah was allowed to join George B. McClellan Post Number Nine, Grand Army of the Republic. She was the only female member.

Her health failed and she succumbed on September 5, 1898 in LaPorte. Former comrades believed that Sarah should be buried in a military cemetery. On May 31, 1901, Sarah's remains were moved to the Grand Army of the Republic plot in Washington Cemetery in Houston, Texas. She is the only woman buried there and her marker reads: "Emma E. Seelye, Army Nurse."

## EMILY

Emily from Brooklyn, New York, expressed a desire to enlist in 1863. Her parents, fearing she was mentally deranged, sent her to her aunt in Michigan. Emily escaped from her aunt's Michigan home and assumed the guise of a boy. She enlisted as a drummer in Van Cleve's Division, Army of the Cumberland, and served in the Tullahoma and Chickamauga campaigns.

Emily became a combat casualty during the Siege of Lookout Mountain. Before dying, she sent a message to her father, "Forgive your dying daughter. I have but a few moments to live. My native soil drinks my blood. I expected to deliver my country but the Fates would not have it so. I am content to die. Pray, Pa, Forgive me. Tell Ma to kiss my daguerreotype. Emily"

## ANNIE ETHERIDGE

Annie Etheridge was born on May 3, 1844, in Detroit, Michigan. While still a child, her family moved to Wisconsin. Her father suffered financial losses and moved back to Detroit when Annie was a young adult. Annie stayed in Wisconsin until she was older. She met her husband while visiting her father. The two were visiting her father in Detroit when the Civil War began. Both enlisted in the 2nd Michigan Infantry but later transferred to the 3rd Michigan Infantry. Three years later, the duo transferred to the 5th Michigan. Annie enlisted as a vivandiere.

Annie was called "Gentle Annie" and "Michigan Annie" by the soldiers she served with. She rode side-saddle with long skirts bedecked with two silver pistols in her belt. She is described as a true heroine with modesty, quiet bearing, and deferential manners.

Annie and her spouse first saw action at the Battle of Blackburn's Ford. She fought with the men in most of the Virginia battle. When Annie first began her work as a vivandiere, she was given a horse, a side-saddle, and saddle bags. She began nursing the wounded, riding among the gunfire at the battle front. She moved among the fallen and encouraged the retreating men. General Berry, her commanding officer, remarked "that Annie was cool and self-possessed under as hot a fire as he ever saw or was exposed to himself."

At night, Annie slept on the ground wrapped in a blanket like the soldiers sleeping around her. She was on the Antietam, Chancellorsville, and Gettysburg battlefields, and was with the troops during Grant's final campaign. Her clothes were torn numerous times by minie balls and shrapnel, but she never received a wound.

Frequently when the battle roared and the troops faltered, Annie would rush forward waving the regimental colors, encouraging the men, and often shaming them with her heroism. In the Battle of the Wilderness, when the fighting reached its apex, several Union regiments were surrounded by Confederate troops. Annie was speaking to an officer when he fell dead at her feet, shot through the heart by a minie ball. Though temporarily stunned by the situation, Annie ran toward what she mistook to be Union soldier. Quickly realizing her error, Annie ran through the front lines, past soldiers firing at her, and into the thicket for safety.

Her exploits were celebrated by newspaper journalists as well as poets. One anonymous poet wrote the following poem:

*To Miss Anna Etheridge*

The Heroine of the War

Hail, heroine of the battle-field!
Sweet angel of a zeal divine!
Hail, maiden, whose device and shield,
Sculptured in tears and prayers, will shine,

On Love's eternal column reared
In memory of the martyred dead,
To be, through coming time, revered,
And sacred to the pilgrim's tread!

Hail, dauntless maid! whose shadowy form,
Borne like a sunbeam on the air,
Swept by amid the battle-storm,
Cheering the helpless sufferers there,

Amid the cannon's smoke and flame,
The earthquake roar of shot and shell,
Winning, by deeds of love, a name
Immortal as the brave who fell.

Hail, angel! whose diviner spell
Charmed dying heroes with her prayer,
Stanching their wounds amid the knell
Of death, destruction, and despair.

Thy name by memory shall be wreathed
Round many desolate hearts in prayer;
By orphan lips it shall be breathed,
And float in songs upon the air.

And History's pages shall embalm
The heroine's deeds in lines of fire;
Her life shall prove a hallowed charm,
And every loyal heart inspire.

Press on, press on! in glory move !
Unfading laurels shall be thine
To gem the victor-crown of Love,
And sparkle in the realms divine!

## FRANK

A young woman from Pittsburgh, Pennsylvania, impersonating a soldier named Frank, enlisted in the 2nd East Tennessee Cavalry in July 1862. Her parents had sent her to a convent in Wheeling, West Virginia when the Civil War began, thinking that would be the safest place for her during the War.

Frank was in the midst of the Battle of Murfreesboro, and was wounded in the shoulder. When the wound was dressed, her secret was revealed. Although she begged General Rosencrans to allow her to stay, the request was denied. Frank was given a military escort provided by Rosencrans, with orders to return her to her father. At Bowling Green, Kentucky, Frank gave her escort the slip. She enlisted in the first troop she came to—the 8th Michigan Volunteers. She became an expert scout and was given the honor of being regimental bugler. In April 1863, Frank accompanied her captain to Louisville, Kentucky, with a band of Confederate prisoners. She made a favorable impression on the local commanding officer, who had her assigned to his regiment.

Frank's cover was blown a few days later when she was recognized by an old family friend. Again, she begged to stay as she had already served ten months. The commander allowed Frank to serve out her term of enlistment. She held the post at Barracks Number One until the War ended.

## ELSA JANE CHARLOTTE GUERIN

Widowed at the age of sixteen, with two young daughters to support, Elsa Jane Charlotte Guerin, also known as Charles Harfield and Mountain Charley, donned her first pair of trousers and became a man. She wore the guises of a sailor on the Mississippi River boats and a mule skinner in Kansas prior to the Civil War. In 1862, Elsa, as Charles, enlisted in the Iowa Cavalry and earned the rank of lieutenant.

In 1864, Charles was wounded in a cavalry charge. She was captured by the Confederates and was exchanged, believing that her gender was revealed by the doctors who treated her. She was amazed to find her secret safe and that she had been promoted to first lieutenant by General Curtis. Charles Hatfield was mustered out in 1865.

Elsa Jane was in male attire for at least fourteen years. She did remarry and occasionally dressed in feminine attire. She wrote later that, "[I] rather like the freedom of my new character...I could go where I chose, do many things I wished to do...."

## JENNIE HODGERS

Irene (Jennie) Hodgers was born in Belfast, Ireland, on December 25, 1844. She came to the United States as a stowaway dressed in male attire. Once in the States, Irene worked as a farm laborer or a shepherd. When the War Between the States began, she enlisted in the 95th Illinois Infantry, Company G, at the age of nineteen, masquerading as Albert J. Cashier. Her company commander was Captain Elliott N. Bush. She chased Major Sterling Price across Missouri and participated in the Battle of Nashville. Irene (Albert) fought in northern Mississippi against Nathan Bedford Forrest. In February 1865, her unit took Fort Blakely in Mobile, Alabama.

She participated in the Red River and Vicksburg Campaigns and the capture of Mobile. Irene fought in forty battles and skirmishes and was never wounded. In August 1865, Cashier's regiment was returned to Camp Butler where it was disbanded. The group received a hero's welcome in Belvediere, Illinois, where the regiment was officially mustered out on August 17, 1865. Irene had fought in an Illinois regiment for four years, all the while maintaining her secret identity. The name of Albert Cashier is etched among the thirty-six thousand three hundred twelve names listed on the Vicksburg, Illinois, monument honoring its Civil War veterans.

In 1869, Irene still in the guise of Albert, settled in Sounemin, Illinois, where she worked as a handyman. In 1899, Albert filed for a veteran's pension and passed a routine medical exam. The examining physician did not know Albert was really a female.

Albert's real identity was discovered when her hip was broken during an automobile accident in 1911. Irene had kept her male disguise for decades. Irene, who at the time was employed by a U. S. senator, was hit by his car as he backed the vehicle out of his driveway. At the age of sixty-six, Irene was too crippled to live alone. Her employer, now former Senator Ira M. Lish, arranged for her admission into the Soldier and Sailor's Home in Quincy, Illinois. Her feminine secret was safe until her senility forced her to be transferred to the Watertown State Hospital for the Insane in March 1913. She continued to collect an invalid soldier's pension of seventy dollars each month.

During a 1914 pension review, one fellow soldier, Harry G. Weaver, signed an affidavit stating:

> When we were examined [at induction] we were not stripped. We were examined the same day. All that we showed was our hands and feet. I never did see any part of his person exposed by which I could determine the sex. He was a very retiring disposition and did not take part in any of the games. He would sit around and watch but would not take part. He had very small hands and feet. He was the smallest man in the company.

A second comrade reported, "Cashier was very quiet in his manner and was not easy to get acquainted with." Many knew (Irene) Albert as a five foot three inch loner who was a good soldier. They knew Albert could keep up on the hardest marches in spite of his small stature. The other soldiers commented that Albert handled a rifle skillfully and never shirked his duty. Tributes were given to Albert for heroism. Gerhard P. Clausius wrote, "In handling a musket in battle, he was able to withstand...the problems of an infantry man as well as his comrades who were bigger and brawnier. If a husky comrade assisted Albert in handling a heavy assignment, Albert would volunteer to help with his chores of washing clothes or replacing buttons. Albert seemed especially adept at those tasks so despised by the infantrymen."

Irene Hodgers, also known as Albert Cashier, died in her sleep on October 11, 1915. A full unit of the Grand Army of the Republic made certain she was buried in her uniform with full military honors at

Sounemin Cemetery. A story in the *Washington Sunday Star* headlined Irene's life. The *Quincy Whig* did a follow-up story. They told of a little woman who believed only a few knew her as a female. Since the story of her extraordinary life has appeared in print, many pictures of her have been preserved by the children and grandchildren of the veterans at the Soldier and Sailor's Home as souvenirs.

## FRANCES HOOK

Frances Hook, as known as Frank Martin, was orphaned at the age of three and sent to live with an older brother in Chicago. When the Civil War began, Frances and her brother enlisted in the 65th Illinois Home Guard. They served three months before being mustered into the 90th Illinois. The young woman had the perfect features to impersonate a soldier. The medium height maid with hazel eyes, dark hair and rounded features deceived everyone.

Frances was taken prisoner during the Battle of Chattanooga. She was searching buildings for food and supplies when captured. Frances' secret was safe until she was wounded in the leg while trying to escape. Her sex was revealed when the wound was treated.

Frances was confined in an Atlanta prison. Jefferson Davis admired her pluck and offered her a Confederate lieutenant's commission if she would join the Confederacy, but Frances respectfully declined. Her Confederate captors wanted to sent her home. They were surprised when she rejected the offer with a sharp retort, "Go home, my only brother was killed at Pittsburg Landing and I have no home— no friends!" They sent her home in feminine attire.

Once on the Union side, Frances tried to enlist in the 19th Illinois but her success or failure is not recorded.

## ANNIE LILLIBRIDGE

Annie Lillibridge (Lillybridge) of Detroit, Michigan, was working in a dry goods store when she met a lieutenant from the 21st Michigan Infantry. The two fell in love and could not bear to be parted, so Annie assumed the persona of a man and joined the 21st. The regiment marched into Kentucky. A few days before the Battle of Pea Ridge, a fellow soldier discovered Annie's gender but she swore him to secrecy. During the battle, Annie killed a Confederate captain who was lining her lover up in the crosshairs of his rifle. The soldier who knew Annie's secret also died at Pea Ridge.

After Pea Ridge, Annie was promoted to regimental clerk by her commander, Colonel Ambrose A. Stevens. The position brought her in close contact with her lover, who had also been promoted, to a major.

On picket duty, a few weeks after Pea Ridge, Annie was shot in the arm. The camp surgeon could not properly care for the wound, so Annie was sent to a Louisville, Kentucky, hospital, where she was hospitalized for several months.

Although Annie was released with a stiff, useless arm, she begged to return to the regiment. The surgeon discharged her and she returned to Cincinnati, Ohio. She swore to reenlist if she could find a recruiter for the 21st Michigan. Annie wanted to be near her lover— for if he fell, she must care for him and if he died, she must die. Annie swapped discharge papers with one Joseph Henderson to be near her lover.

## MADEMOISELLE MAJOR

Captain D. P. Conyngham recorded the adventures of a scout named Bentley in *Sherman's March Through the South*:

At the Battle of Peach Tree Creek (July 20, 1864), I got captured and was brought before General Hood to be pumped, and as he could not get anything out of me, he had ordered me back to the other prisoners, when an officer, attended by an escort, rode up, and saluted the General.

"Ha! Mademoiselle Major, how do you do?" replied the General, doffing his hat.

"Well, General," and she jumped off her horse, throwing the bridle to her orderly and politely returned the salute.

The She-Major was strangely dressed; she wore a cap decked with feathers and gold lace, flowing pants, with a full kind of velvet coat coming just below her hips, and fastened with a rich crimson sash, and partly open at the bosom. In her belt, she carried a revolver, and by her side, a regulation sword. I looked at her; her features were rather sunburned, giving her a manly appearance. Only for her voluptuous bust, little hands, and peculiar airs, I might have taken her to be a very handsome little officer of the masculine gender.

As I gazed at her, she looked full into my face; and turning to the General, she pointed her whip at me and asked, "Who is that fellow, General?"

"A prisoner that has just come in—a dunce, I couldn't get a word out of him."

"Indeed, General, that is a spy," and she again pointed her whip at me. "I saw him at General Johnston's...full of lying information, which cost the General many a life." Her orderly confirmed her accusations of me.

The Mademoiselle Major and General Hood went into his tent. When she came out I was placed between the She-Major and her orderly as they rode out of the camp. Once in the woods, the Major and her orderly dismounted. The Major produced a strong, fine rope from beneath her jacket.

"Sneaking dog of a Yankee, you hung the only man I ever loved; I swore I'd have vengeance. I have had it; but I have it doubly now, by giving you a similar death."

My hands were tied and I was placed back on the horse. The orderly stood over me with his pistols drawn while the Major placed the rope around my neck. The orderly proceeded to climb up the tree with the rope while the Major held the pistols.

I seized the opportunity, jerked the rope with my tied hands, catching the orderly off guard, while kicking my mount with one foot, I buried the other foot in the She-Major's face before she could fire. My mount responded quickly and I escaped to safety, never to fully-trust a woman again.

## MARION MCKINZIE

Marion McKinzie, also known as Harry Fitzallen of the 5th Virginia Volunteers, was born in Nashville but she grew up in Cincinnati. Her male friends provided her with a uniform but her gender was quickly detected. At age twenty, Marion was sent to Athenaeum Prison. After her release, Marion served with another unit.

Official records of the 5th Virginia indicate that Marion was a former actress who enlisted in a Kentucky unit in 1861. She and her colleague, Mary Jane Green, were sent to the Old Capitol Prison when they were captured by Union soldiers. Marion was eventually released and she served in numerous units until the Civil War ended.

## SUE MUNDY

Sue Mundy, also known as Lieutenant Flowers, was an official in a band of irregulars. The group was a remnant of Gen. John Morgan's troop commanded by Captain Berry, with Mundy second in command. The troop operated in Kentucky with their primary duties being the harassment of Federal outposts and the plundering of Union loyalists. Sue took particularly pleasure in relieving loyalists of their jewelry.

Lieutenant Flowers was arrested on espionage charges by the Wisconsin cavalry a few weeks before the Civil War ended. During her incarceration, Flowers confessed to being a female in male attire. Plans were made to trade Sue for other female prisoners when it was discovered that Sue was actually Marcellus Clark.

On March 15, 1865, as Marcellus Clark (also known as Sue Mundy, also known as Lieutenant Flowers) headed for an appointment with the hangman, his dying request was that a large lock of hair be cut from his head and carefully distributed to the men he had commanded. (Hair was valued as a souvenir.) The exploits of Sue Mundy were greatly exaggerated by the *Louisville Daily Journal* but many maintain that Sue Mundy was a very attractive woman.

## MARY OWENS

Mary Owens of Huntington County, also known as John Evans, enlisted in Danville, Montour County, Pennsylvania, to be with her husband. Her husband was killed and Mary was wounded in the same battle. Mary remained in service for eighteen months and actively participated in three major battles. She was wounded twice, once above the right eye and once in the arm. The second wound was serious enough to require medical attention, her sex was discovered, and Mary was sent home. The local press celebrated Mary's return and called her "the heroine of the neighborhood."

## BETTIE TAYLOR PHILLIPS

Bettie Taylor Phillips was born to Dr. Gibson Bury Taylor and Mary Rives Taylor on April 6, 1830, in Morganfield, Kentucky. She married W. D. Phillips in 1847. When her spouse joined the 4th Kentucky Infantry as a quartermaster in the fall of 1861, Bettie went with him. She became known as the mother of the "Orphan Brigade...in camp, on long marches, often under shot and shell of the enemy." The Orphan Brigade was so named because the State of Kentucky refused to recognize them as an official unit. The group was organized and trained in Tennessee.

Bettie and her husband fought in the Battle of Shiloh. After two years of active duty, Bettie's health deteriorated and she was sent home to recuperate. While traveling home, Bettie was arrested by Union soldiers in Nashville, Tennessee. When the soldiers tried to search her, Bettie pulled her pistol and snorted, "Stop where you are! I will never submit to the humiliation of being searched by men. Send a woman to me." A woman was sent for as the soldiers retreated.

She was sent to Louisville, Kentucky, to be tried for conspiracy and espionage. She was acquitted and released. Bettie, fully rested from her month of incarceration, returned to the Orphan Brigade upon her release. She stayed with the unit until the war was over. After the war, Bettie returned to Uniontown, Kentucky. It is not recorded whether or not her husband accompanied her. Bettie later served as the promoter of the soldier's monument which was erected at Morganfield, Kentucky.

# ELLA RENO

Journal entries of Daniel Reed Larned, private secretary to General Ambrose Burnside, recorded in detail on May 14, 1863, the discovery of a cavalryman in the 5th Kentucky. He was a she, named Ella Reno, the niece of General Jesse Lee Reno. Larned indicated Reno had served eighteen months and that she was noted for her bravery and daring. Ella Reno was dressed in feminine attire to be sent home. Reno stated that she had been sent home on three different occasions but that she had returned and she would do so again.

His entry for the following day, stated that he could not understand how Ella had passed for a man. He also recounted her military career:

> She served four months as a private in the 5th Kentucky Cavalry—was then transferred by her own request to the 8th Michigan Infantry and has done all of the duties of ordinary private; made long marches, been in hot battles, stood guard, been out on picket duty, and was admonished for telling her superior officer that "if he were not more loyal he had better take off his stripes, throw up his commission and go home,"—was put in prison and did prison duty for two weeks, went out foraging on a mule, was ordered to take a train of wagons around a river at night which she accomplished.

He reiterated Reno's commitment to rejoin the troops but personally doubted her ability to do so, and wrote that Burnside had procured Reno a position in a Louisville hospital.

# BELLE REYNOLDS

Arabella "Belle" Macomber was born on October 20, 1840, in Shelurne Falls, Massachusetts. Belle married Lieutenant Reynolds of Peoria, Illinois, on April 17, 1860. When his regiment shipped out to Bird's Point, Missouri, on August 10, 1861, Belle went with him. She kept one of the best records of army life during the Civil War. Belle wrote of the desolation and despair of army camp life.

During the winter of 1862, Belle traveled with the regiment from South Missouri to the Mississippi River. She had no regular conveyance and often rode in an army wagon or on a mule. Occasionally, she marched with the soldiers. Although this portion of Belle's military service was not dangerous, it was busy, filling her days with the romance of wilderness life.

When Lieutenant Reynolds led his troops into their first conflict, the Battle of Belmont, Belle was not allowed to leave the camp. Her journal entry records her anguish and fear for her spouse. When he safely re-

***Belle Reynolds.***
(The Western Reserve Histirical Society)

turned to her, her writing is jubilant that he is safe but she grieves over the losses other mothers and wives will be forced to endure.

Belle and her husband spent the remainder of the winter stationed at Cape Girardeau. In February 1862, Grant began to move troops into the upper Mississippi Valley and the 17th Illinois was one of the regiments. Belle was in the heat of battle when Corinth and Memphis were captured. Her writings record the first day of fighting at Pittsburg Landing. Belle mixes the beauty of the region with the horrors of war when she writes in her journal.

On April 17, 1862, the camp of the 17th Illinois was overrun by Confederates and Belle had to retreat rapidly. Cannonballs tore through the camp ripping tents and flesh alike. The soldiers and Belle feared for their lives. Only when they reached the *Emerald*, the floating headquarters of Captain Norton, was their anxiety reduced.

Belle's journal entries describe the deafening sound of artillery fire, the shot falling around the soldiers like hail during a summer shower. She describes the pain and suffering of the wounded and the jubilation of the victorious. Belle describes the panic and terror of the retreat and the suspense and agony of being separated from her husband—not knowing the state of his being.

Belle records her joy in being reunited with her husband. Although conditions were uncomfortable and the elements forbidding, Belle chose to remain with him throughout the conflict. In spite of cold, rainy weather, sleeping on the ground, without protection, being forced to dodge mortar rounds and minie balls, Belle always managed to season her journal entries with the beauty of the area such as blooming magnolias or cherry trees.

After Vicksburg fell, Belle and her lieutenant were stationed at Milliken's Bend for a brief time and then moved into Vicksburg where they spent several quiet months. Lieutenant Reynolds' military career ended in May 1864, and the inseparable couple gratefully returned to the solitude of civilian life after four years of adventure and danger.

## BETTY SULLIVAN

Betty Sullivan, like so many other wives followed her husband, John, into battle. When Company K, 1st Tennessee Infantry Regiment was organized at Pulaski in May 1861, Betty and John were the first to enlist, and Betty became known as "Mother Sullivan." Not only did Betty march with the men, she cared for the wounded as well as kept their uniforms clean and mended.

The regiment marched first to West Virginia and then into northern Virginia. The group was under the command of General Stonewall Jackson. "She [Betty] marched on foot with her knapsack on her back through the mountains of West Virginia, slept on the frozen ground, under the cold skies, a blanket her only covering, her knapsack, her pillow."

In 1862, she fought with the troops at Shiloh, Corinth, and Perryville, Kentucky. When her husband was wounded at Perryville, Betty left the front lines to care for him. When General Braxton Bragg left Kentucky, the wounded were left at Harrisburg. All of them, including Betty, were taken prisoner by the advancing Union Army. The wounded were transported to a nearby prison, where Betty continued to care for the wounded, including her spouse.

No record remains of Betty and John Sullivan's lives after their release from the Union prison.

## SARAH TAYLOR

Captain Sarah Taylor was the regimental daughter for the 1st Tennessee Infantry. She was the step-daughter of Captain Dowden. Sarah envisioned herself as a Tennessee Joan of Arc.

Sarah rode into her first battle at the age of eighteen. She had a cocky little blue hat over her long dark tresses. On her belt, Sarah carried silver mounted pistols and a regulation sword. She was an expert with both saber and shot. Sarah rode into battle courageously, relying on her equestrian skills as well as her marksmanship. The soldiers felt they could not lose with Captain Sarah in the lead.

## MARIE TEPE

Marie Tepe was known to the soldiers as "French Mary." She joined Company One of the 27th Pennsylvania Volunteers (Washington's Brigade) with her husband on April 16, 1861. Marie operated a profitable sutler trade specializing in contraband whiskey. She drew regular soldier's wages plus twenty-five cents a day extra for hospital services, earning a total of $21.25 per month.

Marie was in the heat of battle fourteen times from the First Battle of Bull Run through the Peninsula Campaign, and was recognized for outstanding service. Marie was assigned to Col. Charles H. T. Collis, commander of the 114th Pennsylvania Volunteers (known as Collis' Zouaves d'Afrique). She was wounded in the left ankle by a minie ball. General Phillip Kearny awarded Marie the Kearny Cross for her heroism under fire.

After recuperating, Marie returned to the 114th Pennsylvania. She remained with them through 1864, surviving the Battles of Gettysburg, the Wilderness, Spotsylvania, Cold Harbor, 2nd Bull Run, Richmond, and Chancellorsville.

Marie wore a blue Zouave jacket with a short red skirt over a pair of red trousers and boots. A nautical style hat with the brim turned down kept her curls in place.

Frank Rauscher mentioned her in his diary on October 27, 1862, when he wrote that, "Nearly all the men fell head along into the channel and stumbled over the large stones, becoming wringing wet. All were in the same predicament, excepting the staff officers, who were on horseback, and Marie, the vivandiere, who had the forethought to pick up an old mule, on which she safely crossed the river."

*Marie Tepe.*

## LUCY MATILDA THOMPSON

Lucy Matilda Thompson was born on November 21, 1812, in Bladenbow, North Carolina, to Duncan Thompson, a member of the Waccamau Indian tribe. Lucy was agile and strong by the age of seventeen. She was an expert horseman and marksman.

At the age of forty-nine, Lucy married Bryant Gauss. When Bryant joined the 18th North Carolina Infantry (Bladen Light Infantry) Regiment, Lucy was determined not to be left behind. "She cut her thick hair very close, remodeled Bryant's suit to fit herself, oiled her squirrel musket and went off to enlist," as recorded by the National Women's Military Museum. Lucy became known as Private Bill Thompson. If the neighbors knew, they kept quiet. If Lucy's commanding officers, Captain Robert Tate and Lieutenant Wiley Sikes, knew of Lucy's secret, nothing was ever said.

At the First Battle of Bull Run, Lucy received a wound that tore her scalp open from the forehead to the crown. She spent two months in the hospital, with her wound protected by a metal plate. Lucy's gender was discovered during her convalescence. She was wounded again later, in the Siege of Richmond.

Bryant was wounded four times, mortally near Mechanicsville during the Seven Days' Battle. Lucy requested a furlough and took her departed husband home for burial.

Lucy gave birth to a child in January 1864, at the age of fifty-one. She stayed in North Carolina for the remainder of the war. Lucy later married Joseph Patrick Henry Kenny, a Union veteran. The couple had six children, the last of which was born when Lucy was sixty-eight.

Joseph died in 1913, at the age of 107. Lucy's military record was told to her pastor in 1914. She quickly became a celebrity, giving interviews as late as her one hundred ninth birthday. Lucy died on June 22, 1925, at the age of one hundred twelve. She was buried at Meeks Cemetery near Nicholls, Georgia, next to her second husband.

## NADINE BASIS TURCHIN

Madame Nadine Basil Turchin, the daughter of a Russian commander of the Czar's Regiment, married a Russian officer named John Turchin. The newlyweds moved to the United States and John enlisted as a Union officer, a colonel in the 19th Illinois. Nadine enlisted, too, serving first as a nurse and aide-de-camp to her husband.

In April 1862, Colonel Turchin became very ill during a march to Tennessee. He traveled in an ambulance for weeks. Madame Turchin assumed her husband's command. Her command was so judicious that her orders were obeyed promptly without complaints or threats of mutiny. Madame Turchin rode into battle on a large horse, sitting in her sidesaddle, stern, ladylike, and larger-than-life, constantly under fire. She cared for the fallen while threatening, cajoling, and rallying her warriors. Madame Turchin "always manifested the most perfect indifference to the shot and shell or the whizzing minie balls that fell around her. She seemed entirely devoid of fear, and though constantly exposed to the enemy's fire, never received even a scratch," wrote one young soldier to his mother.

After the colonel recovered, he encouraged his troops to ravage Athens, Alabama. His superiors were appalled, and he was court-martialed. Madame Turchin in true form rushed to her spouse's rescue. She boarded a train bound for Washington. Her skillful manipulations had the court-martial proceedings dismissed and her husband promoted to brigadier-general, much to the chagrin of his accusers.

Turchin performed admirably at Chickamauga and earned the nickname "Russian Thunderbolt." He also led his troops at Missionary Ridge and through the Atlanta Campaign.

Poor health forced the only Russian Union officer into retirement, and Madame Turchin joined him. They returned to their home at Kenwood, Illinois, where they worked as immigration agents for the Illinois Central Railroad. They then moved to Radom, Illinois, where they established a colony of Polish immigrants. The general died in 1901, but Madame Turchin refused his pension. She rejoined her husband on July 17, 1904.

## LORETA JANITA VELAZQUEZ

Loreta Janita Velazquez was born on June 26, 1842, in Havana, Cuba, the daughter of Cuban aristocracy. In her early teens, Loreta married an American merchant named Roch, who had strong financial holdings in Cuba. Roch joined the Confederate army when the War Between the States began. He was soon killed, although not in a combat situation. The grief-stricken Loreta swore revenge on the Yankees, believing they were responsible for her husband's early demise.

Loreta disguised herself as Lieutenant Harry Buford. She cut her dark hair short and glued on a false mustache and goatee. Loreta spoke in a deep voice, walked with a masculine swagger, and even spat on the streets. She flirted with several young women to complete her disguise. She used her family's wealth to equip a company called the "Arkansas Grays," and took command as Lieutenant Harry Buford. Her own commander was General Barnard Bee.

Harry led her troops into the Battles of Bull Run and Ball's Bluff in 1861. She took command of a second company at Ball's Bluff when all

*Loreta Velazquez.*      (Library of Congress)

of the officers were critically wounded or dead. Harry later led her troops into the Battles of Fort Donelson, Shiloh, and Fort Pillow. She was wounded in the foot during a skirmish on February 13, 1862, on the Cumberland River, and was sent to New Orleans to recuperate. Her secret was safe.

After a brief recovery, Harry was sent to the 21st Louisiana where she led patrols. On one occasion, a shrapnel shell burst above her troops, killing one man and wounding Harry in the chest and right arm, knocking her from her horse. With assistance, Harry climbed back onto her mount and led her patrol out of harm's way. Her wounds were dressed in the field and she was then evacuated to the Corinth, Mississippi, hospital.

Knowing her secret would be revealed, Loreta admitted her gender to the surgeon and begged him not to report her. The surgeon was a true Southern gentleman and did not reveal the lady's secret but secured private treatment for her. It is not known if the surgeon received monetary compensation from Loreta for his assistance.

After returning to her troops a second time, she grew bored with the inactivity of the military waiting game and left her troops in the command of a provost marshal. She procured a wardrobe of assorted costumes and infiltrated Union military camps in order to gain beneficial information. She even met with Abraham Lincoln's chief detective, Lafayette C. Baker, and enlisted as an agent for the North. Little did the Union officers know, Loreta's luggage was lined with messages and funds for the Canadian Confederate agents.

Upon arrival in the Northwest Territory, Loreta was afraid the Canadian agents might reveal her true colors, but they held fast and her activities as a double agent were not revealed. She helped to instigate a prison insurrection which was successful and the Confederate prisoners escaped, although it did not appear that Loreta had anything to do with it.

After the War, Loreta recorded her exploits in an 1876 publication entitled, *The Woman In Battle: A Narrative Of The Exploits, Adventures, And Travels Of Madame Loreta Janeta Velazquez, Otherwise Known As Lieutenant Harry T. Buford, Confederate States Army.*

General Jubal Early was incensed by Loreta's writings, especially her claims of serving as a Confederate officer. However, records housed at Castle Thunder Prison supported Loreta's military adventures. Richmond newspapers sang Lieutenant Buford's praises during the Civil War.

After the War Between the States, Loreta remarried a very wealthy Southern gentleman, Major Wesson. The remainder of her life with Wesson was spent in travel abroad. Wesson died in Caracas, Venezuela.

Loreta married a third time to a Nevada gentleman of means. A son was born to them while they resided in Salt Lake City, Utah. History could not keep up with Loreta and she disappeared in the late 1870s. As the name of her last husband is not known, Loreta became very hard to trace.

## SARAH ROSETTA WAKEMAN

Sarah Rosetta Wakeman was born on January 18, 1843, near Big Hampton, New York, the oldest of nine children. At nineteen, Sarah ran away from home and assumed the disguise of a male, Pat Lyons. With little education, Sarah could only secure a position as a canal boatman on the Chenango Canal.

Sarah enlisted in the 153rd New York State Volunteers, Company G, on August 30, 1862, at Fonda, Montgomery County, New York. She was given $152.00 for enlisting which she sent home. She wrote letters home telling the family of her exploits but her soldiering pained her family. She joined the army because she was "tired of staying in that neighborhood." Sarah is described as five feet tall with fair complexion, blue eyes, and brown hair.

On October 18, 1862, Sarah was stationed in Alexandria, Virginia, with the regiment to protect the capital. The group was soon transported by boat to Louisiana. Sarah participated in the Red River Campaign. On one occasion, Sarah climbed on top of a pile of downed trees, stood as tall as her five foot frame could stand, and shouted to a group of Confederates, "Hey! You darn Rebels, why don't you get up where we can see you?" She picked up the fallen Union flag and placed it on the tallest tree.

Sarah sent money home to help her father pay off the farm debts. Her letters described her military life: boredom, homesickness, fear, anticipation, and bravado. She wrote home that, "If it is God's will for me to be killed here, it is my will to die." Her letter was postmarked Alexandria, Virginia.

Sarah had a fist fight with a fellow soldier named Stephen Wiley. Exactly what caused the fight or who won is unknown but Sarah wrote home, "[he] pitched on me and I gave him three or four good cracks and he put downstairs with himself."

Sarah fought at Pleasant Hill and wrote home of the battle, "There was heavy cannonading all day and a sharp firing of the infantry...I was not in the first day's fight but the next day I had to face the enemy's bullets with my regiment. I was under fire about four hours and lay on the field of battle all night. There were three wounded in my company and one killed."

The regiment marched to Mississippi by way of North Carolina. Along the way, Sarah was felled by chronic diarrhea. She was transported to a New Orleans military hospital where she died on June 9, 1864, some two years after her enlistment. Sarah was buried in grave #711 in the Monument Cemetery in New Orleans. Her headstone is inscribed, "Lyons Wakeman, New York." Sarah's letters to home are in the possession of Ruth Gadier, Sarah's great niece.

## ELIZA WILSON

Eliza Wilson was twenty-one when she enlisted in the 5th Wisconsin to serve as their vivandiere. As the daughter of a wealthy Menomonie, Wisconsin family, Eliza had a large volume of supplies at her disposal. Eliza wore a Turkish-style costume with a brown waltz-length skirt over bloomers, morocco shoes and black hat with matching plumes. She stayed with the 5th Wisconsin until the regiment mustered out.

The Wisconsin Historical Society Archives has a letter from L. D. Culver, a soldier in the 5th Wisconsin who wrote of Eliza:

We have not seen a woman for a fortnight with the exception of the Daughter of the Regiment, who is with us in storm and sunshine. It would do you good to see her trudging along, with or after the regiment, her dark brown frock buttoned tightly around her waist, her what-you-call-ems tucked into her well-fitted gaiters, her hat and feather set jauntily on one side, her step firm and assured, for she knows that every arm in our ranks would protect her. Never pouting or passionate, with a kind word for everyone, and every one a kind word for her.

## FANNIE WILSON

Fannie Wilson and her friend Nellie Graves, both nineteen years old and from Williamsburg, New York, schemed to enlist in the Union Army. Nellie and Fannie fought in the Union military for eighteen months until Nellie was wounded at Vicksburg. Her secret was discovered by the Confederates who treated her injuries. They returned her to the Union officers with the following message, "As the Confederates do not use women in the War, this woman, wounded in battle, is returned to you." When Nellie was asked why she enlisted, her retort was, "I thought I'd like camp life and I did."

Fannie fell ill and was sent to a Cairo, Illinois, hospital to recover. Once her health returned, Fannie danced in the local ballet to raise funds for the Sanitary Commission. She later reenlisted in the 3rd Illinois Cavalry where she served until August 1864 when she was arrested for being in improper attire (a soldier's uniform).

*Seige of Vicksburg.*                              (Library of Congress)

*Many other women, with contributions just as significant as those on the previous pages, but for whom there is but little documentation, served with valor on the battlefields of war. It is fitting that they be recognized in this work.*

## CHARLOTTE ANDERSON

Charlotte Anderson of Cleveland, Ohio, joined the 60th Ohio Infantry as Charley Anderson. On January 18, 1865, Provost Marshal General Marsena Patrick interviewed Charley at City Point, Virginia, and ascertained that Charley was actually Charlotte. In spite of loud protests, Charlotte was returned to her home four days after the interview—in female attire.

## MRS. JOHN BAKR

Mrs. John Bakr, also known as "She Bear" (her husband was called "He Bear") served as a vivandiere for the Washington Artillery of New Orleans, Louisiana. Her uniform was provided by their commander, Colonel Slocomb, who personally designed it.

## MOLLIE BEAN

Mollie Bean mustered into the 47th North Carolina Infantry. She served two years before being wounded, when her sex was revealed. Mollie was arrested and imprisoned at Castle Thunder. A North Carolina newspaper recorded her arrest, "...that common receptacle of the guilty, the suspected, and the unfortunate. This poor creature is, from her record, manifestly crazy."

## MADAME BOIVERT

Madame Boivert and Mary Ann Perkins were listed on the military rolls of Gordes LaFayette from Mobile, Alabama.

## HARRIET BROWN

Harriett Brown enlisted in an Illinois regiment as Harry Brown. She served for three months before her gender was discovered. Harry was arrested in Chicago while wearing a Union uniform, relieved of military service and sent to a military hospital to serve as a nurse.

## MARY BURNS

Mary Burns, also known as John Burns, enlisted in the 7th Michigan Cavalry to be near her boyfriend. Her gender was discovered about ten days after her enlistment and she was sent home. According to the Detroit *Advertiser And Tribune*, dated February 25, 1864, Mary Burns was arrested for impersonating a soldier. The Detroit unit had not been deployed when Mary was apprehended.

## CANADIAN LOU

The *Memphis Bulletin*, dated December 18, 1862, reported "a woman formerly extensively known in this city as 'Canadian Lou' was arrested in this city last night dressed in men's clothes. She was put in jail for inebriety. She was with a Missouri unit on its recent march from this city of Holly Springs and back."

## FRANCES CLALIN

Frances Clalin served three months in Company I, 44th Missouri Artillery and nineteen months in Company A, 13th Missouri Cavalry. Her exploits are unknown.

## SARAH COLLINS

Private Sarah Collins from Lake Mills, Wisconsin, enlisted in the 1st Kentucky Infantry with her brother. She never made it into battle. Her sex was detected because of the way she put on her socks and shoes. When she was discharged, Federal officials arrested her on suspicion of being a Confederate spy. She was sent to Columbus, Ohio, for trial but was never indicted or imprisoned.

## LIZZIE COMPTON

Lizzie Compton of London, Canada, enlisted at the age of fourteen. She served in seven different units of the Army of the Potomac and the Cumberland Army during an eighteen month period. She would leave one, and join a different one when her secret was discovered due to wounds.

Lizzie was first wounded at the Battle of Fredericksburg. At the Battle of Green River, she was wounded severely enough that she was forced into several months of inactivity so she could recuperate.

# LUCY ANN COX

Lucy Ann Cox enlisted with her husband in the 104th New York and the 14th Virginia as a vivandiere. She saw action as a color bearer and a nurse.

# SOPHIA CRYER

Sophia Cryer enlisted in the Summer Rifles. Her secret was revealed by an old family friend who exposed Sophia after a week of duty. She was mustered out of the 11th Pennsylvania Infantry, Company A.

# CATHERINE E. DAVIDSON

Catherine E. Davidson of Sheffield, Ohio, enlisted in the 28th Ohio to be with her fiancee. He was mortally wounded at Antietam. She also received a wound but her sex was not revealed. She worked as an assistant to Pennsylvania Governor Andrew Curtin. Curtin did not realize Catherine was a female until she visited him after she had mustered out.

# AMELIA DAVIS

Amelia Davis, the wife of a Baltimore seaman, joined the Confederate Navy with her spouse. They were assigned to duty on the *Red Rover*. The steamer was captured during the Battle for Island 10 in April 1862. The couple were imprisoned for a short time at Camp Douglas in Chicago.

# FRANCES DAY

Frances Day followed her lover, William Fitzpatrick, off to war. Frances enlisted as Sergeant Frank Mayne of the 126th Pennsylvania, Company F. William was killed about thirty days after Frances' enlistment. Frances deserted and Frank Mayne was officially listed as a deserter on August 24, 1862. She moved to Company C and was killed in battle. Her secret was revealed by a burial detail.

# MRS. L. L. DEMING

Mrs. L. L. Deming served with the Tenth Michigan Infantry.

## MARY W. DENNIS

Six foot, two inch tall Mary W. Dennis was one of the few women to win a commission. Her size made her a formidable figure in the Stillwell Company, 1st Minnesota.

## MRS. ELLIS

Mrs. Ellis, the wife of the First Missouri Regiment commander, was a hardriding lady who was in charge of military dispatches. She wore an ornate uniform highlighted with a red sash. Mrs. Ellis was an exceptional shot and carried matching silver pistols in her belt, although orderlies escorted her wherever she went.

## HANNAH EWBANK

Hannah Ewbank, a Marquetter school teacher, marched with the 7th Wisconsin Infantry, as their regimental daughter and vivandiere. Mustered into the regiment on September 2, 1861, Hannah fought at Antietam, Chancellorsville, Fredericksburg, and Gettysburg. She was clad in a blue Zouave jacket accented by a red skirt and white vest and pantaloons. The entire ensemble was trimmed with gold braid. White boots and gloves along with a gold plumbed blue velvet hat completed the outfit.

## AMANDA COLBURN FANHAM

The widow Amanda Colburn Fanham from St. Johnsbury, Vermont, left her child with her parents and enlisted in the 3rd Vermont Regiment to be with her brother. She fought in the Seven Days' Battle before her sex was discovered. Amanda went into nursing after her gender was discovered. She was with Clara Barton at Fairfax. Amanda procured a pass and an ambulance from Secretary Stanton, a practically impossible accomplishment, and worked as a vivandiere and nurse for the remainder of the war.

## ELIZABETH CAIN FINNAN

Elizabeth Cain Finnan served in an Indiana unit as a private, fighting in several battles before her sex was discovered. Elizabeth chose to remain with her regiment as a vivandiere. She died July 25, 1907, at the age of sixty.

## AUGUSTA FOSTER

Augusta Foster from Maine impersonated a male and enlisted. Her military duty was cut short when her mount was shot out from under her at the First Battle of Bull Run. She escaped to Alexandria, Virginia, where she nursed her wounds in safety and solitude.

## MARY GALLOWAY

Clara Barton, on the tour circuit, often told of a female soldier named Mary Galloway. Mary enlisted with her husband, posing as his brother. She was wounded at Antietam, and Clara cared for her at the Poffenberger Farm. Barton did not reveal Mary's secret. So grateful were the Galloways to her that they named their first child Clara.

## ELLA HOBERT GIBSON

Ella Hobert Gibson was appointed chaplain for the First Wisconsin Artillery in 1864, a position she held for twelve months. Ella was the only woman during the War Between the States to hold such a post.

## ELLEN GOODRIDGE

Ellen Goodridge of Wisconsin wanted to accompany her Union fiancee, Lt. James Hendrick, into battle. Ellen's parents disowned her. The lovers fought side by side through the Virginia battles for forty-eight months. Ellen was wounded in the arm by a minie ball and James was felled by disease. He was taken to a hospital in Washington. Ellen stayed with him as his condition deteriorated. A local preacher recited the wedding vows for the dying soldier and his soon to be widow.

## NELLIE GRAVES

Nellie Graves and Fannie Wilson plotted a way to enlist in the Union army. They fought in the Federal regiments for about eighteen months until Nellie was wounded at Vicksburg. Her secret was discovered by the Confederates who treated her injuries. They returned her to the Union officers with the following message, "As the Confederates do not use women in the War, this woman, wounded in battle, is returned to you." When Nellie was asked why she enlisted, her retort was, "I thought I'd like camp life and I did."

## Edward O. Hamilton

The drummer for the 18th New York Infantry was named Edward O. Hamilton. Edward, it seemed, was a tomboy who preferred masculine attire to feminine. Her father had raised her as a boy, the son he never had.

## Mary Hancock

Mary Hancock, a school teacher motivated by an intense dislike of slavery, joined an Illinois regiment as a male. Her future exploits were not recorded.

## Charles Hargield

General Samuel R. Curtis' adjutant had a young orderly named Charles Hargield. Charles turned out to be a twelve year old girl. Charles was commended for her excellent discipline and manners.

## Mary Henry

Mary Henry and Mary Wright were Southern ladies who were arrested in uniform two weeks before Lee's surrender at Appomatox. The "dashing creatures" were captured by the Union army and imprisoned in Nashville until the war's end.

## Bidget Higgins

Bidget Higgins enlisted with her spouse in a Confederate artillery unit in October 1861. The two were taken prisoner during the fall of Island 10 in April 1862. They were sent to the Federal prison in Chicago where they served eight months.

## Mary Hill

Mary Hill, a vivandiere, was noted as being highly respected by all who knew her. This is the only record of Mary Hill.

## Jane Hindale

Mrs. Jane Hindale enlisted in the Second Michigan Artillery and was captured at Blackburn's Ford. She was sent to Bull Run where she begged the Confederate officers to release her. She then made her way to another Federal regiment.

## LUCINDA HORNE

Lucinda Horne, a vivandiere for Company K, 14th South Carolina volunteers, went to war with her husband and son. She left her home in Edgefield County and saw action on several battle fronts.

## KATE W. HOWE

Kate W. Howe, as known as Tom Smith, was the granddaughter of General Winfield Scott. She enlisted as a drummer at the Battle of Lookout Mountain. When she was wounded, her gender was discovered and she was sent home. Kate drew a soldier's pension of $17.00 a month after her discharge.

## SATRONIA SMITH HUNT

Satronia Smith Hunt signed on with her spouse, in an Iowa regiment. He was killed in battle but she remained until their unit was mustered out.

## MARY JANE JACKSON

Mary Jane Jackson (also recorded as Johnson) was orphaned at age sixteen when a cannonball exploded in her home. She felt a need to enlist and she joined the 11th Kentucky Cavalry. Mary Jane served in the Union Army eleven months before her sex was discovered. She was sent to Richmond for deportation to the North.

## MARY OWEN STEVENS JENKINS

Mary Owen Stevens Jenkins joined the 9th Pennsylvania Cavalry. During her two years of active duty, she was wounded but she managed to muster out without her gender being discovered.

## CHARLES JOHEHOUS

The *National Tribune* on May 13, 1886, recorded the disinterment of Federal corpuses near Resca, Georgia, "A body drew attention because of the small feet, upon examination the corpse was a female, shot through the head. The grave was marked, 'Charles Johehous, Private 6th, Missouri.'"

## ANNIE JONES

Annie Jones served as a vivandiere for a New York regiment. Although she saw action on several battlefields, Annie was never wounded.

## LIZZIE JONES

Lizzie Jones served as a regimental daughter for the 6th Massachusetts Volunteers. It was her duty to procure supplies from strawberries to weaponry. She was given a uniform made by Sergeant Crowley. It was a dark velvet jacket with gold lace trim over a red, white, and blue silk skirt. A white hat with red and white plumes highlighted the ensemble. The outfit was accentuated with a silver canteen, which Lizzie wore on her belt. Lizzie was ten years old when she accepted the position of regimental daughter.

## ABREE KAMOO

Abree Kamoo, also known as Tommy Kamoo, was born in Tunis in 1815. She attended the University of Heidelberg in Germany. In 1862, she came to the United States and joined the Union Army. At the age of forty-seven, Tommy was slightly wounded in the nose at Gettysburg. She died in a Boston hospital in 1904.

## KATE

The soldiers of the 116th Illinois knew of Kate's gender but they allowed her to stay because she was such a good fighter. Jesse Reid of the 4th South Carolina wrote home in June 1861 of a female named Kate who dressed as a soldier and served in the 116th Illinois: "Henry C. Bear of the 116th Illinois described his lieutenant, who kept a woman, Kate, dressed in soldier's clothes...You could hardly tell her from a man."

## BARBARA ANN MALPASS

Barbara Ann Malpass assumed the persona of Charles R. Williams and she served in several Union units.

## JULIA MARCUM

Julia Marcum was discovered to be a female after serving several months in a Kentucky unit. The only record of Julia is recorded in Ida Tarbell's letter which is in the National Archives in Washington, D. C.

## CHARLES MARTIN

Charles Martin enlisted in a Pennsylvania regiment as a drummer. He exhibited a good education and excellent manners, and made himself useful as a clerk to officers. He participated in five battles. He fell sick with typhoid fever and was taken to a Pennsylvania hospital, where an alert matron discovered that Charles Martin was actually a girl in her teens.

## MARY McCREARY

Mary McCreary joined Company H, 21st Ohio as a private to be with her spouse. After several months of duty, Mary found herself to be in the "family way." She requested a leave from her commanding officer which was granted. Mary was sent home, never to return to service.

## CHARLEY MILER

Charley Miler had dressed in a masculine manner since childhood. She served with the 18th New York Regimental as a drummer.

## MADILINE MOORE

Like Annie Lillibridge, Madiline Moore followed her lover into battle. Madiline took the uniform of a dead lieutenant and quickly assumed command of a Virginia regiment. She was granted a commission before her sex was discovered. Madiline also led a charge in the Battle of the Wilderness. Her exploits were celebrated in an 1867 autobiography.

*The Battle of the Wilderness.*          (Library of Congress)

## LaBelle Morgan

La Belle Morgan fought with a Michigan unit before her gender was discovered.

## Mary Ann Murphy

Mary Ann Murphy assumed the persona of Samuel Hill and joined Company B, 53rd Massachusetts Infantry. She served with her brother Tom. Author Martha Carolina Keller described the two soldiers who fought at Gettysburg, "The older protected the younger while he slept after the battle. Their fellow comrades believed they were father and son when in all actuality they were brother and sister.

## Nellie A. K.

Nellie A. K., from Long Island, New York, enlisted in the 102nd New York Infantry with her brother. She saw action at Antietam, Chancellorsville, Gettysburg, and Lookout Mountain. Her gender was revealed and she was sent home. Nellie begged Pauline Cushman, the famous Union spy, to help her to reenlist. Whether there was assistance given is unknown. It is also unknown whether Nellie was able to enlist in another regiment.

## Elizabeth Niles

Elizabeth Niles enlisted with her spouse, Martin, in the 4th New York Infantry. They were on their honeymoon when Fort Sumpter fell. Elizabeth cut her hair and the two became soldiers. They fought side by side in several conflicts. Elizabeth died at the age of ninety-two on October 4, 1920.

## Araminta Palmer

Araminta Palmer, a recent widow of a Columbus, Kentucky, Confederate, enlisted as a vivandiere for a Kentucky regiment. The unit was on Island 10 when it fell into Federal hands on April 1862. She was imprisoned at Camp Douglas in Chicago until the officials could release her in their prisoner exchange program.

## Rebecca Parish

Twenty-eight year old Rebecca Parish enlisted with her husband in a Lee County, Georgia unit. Her brother was also mustered into the same unit. The three were captured during the Battle for Island 10 in April 1862. They were imprisoned and Private Parish died while incarcerated. Rebecca and her brother were released several months later.

## BELLE PATTERSON

Belle Patterson enlisted in a Northern regiment in 1862. It is recorded that she made "a fine-looking soldier, and that no one would have suspected she was a female."

## MELVERINA ELVERINA PEPPERCORN

Melverina Elverina Peppercorn, twin sister of Alexander "the Great" Peppercorn, followed him into battle in 1862. They fought side by side until Alexander was wounded. Melverina cared for her wounded sibling. General Lee surrendered before the twins saw additional action.

## MARY ANN PERKINS

Mary Ann Perkins and Madame Boivert were listed on the military rolls of Gordes LaFayette from Mobile, Alabama.

## GEORGIANA PETERMAN

Georgiana Peterman from Ellensboro, Wisconsin, enlisted as a drummer in the 7th Wisconsin Infantry. At age nineteen, she was mustered out after twenty-four months of service. She was an expert with a rifle.

## BELLE PETERSON

Belle Peterson enlisted in a Union unit in September 1862. She served undetected until her unit was mustered out. Many historians have tried to make Georgiana Peterman and Belle Peterson the same person. Mary Livermore recorded both ladies in her book, *My Story Of The War*. She indicated that Belle and Georgiana were two separate people.

## MARY ANN PITTMAN

Mary Ann Pittman, also known as Lieutenant Rawley, from Chestnut Bluff, Tennessee, served under General Nathan Bedford Forrest. As an effective witness, Lieutenant Rawley testified in the 1864 hearing in which the Sons of Liberty were accused of conspiring to oust the United States government.

## HARRIET REDD

Harriett Redd of Pike County, Alabama, enlisted with her husband. The twenty-four year old Harriett, a bride of two years, was left an invalid from wounds received during the Battle for Island 10 in April 1862. Her spouse refused to leave his fallen wife and the two were taken prisoner by Union troops. They were sent to Camp Douglas in Chicago where they made their home.

## IDA REMINGTON

Ida Remington served as an officer's orderly in the 11th New York Infantry from Rochester, New York. Remington was arrested on August 27, 1863, in Harrisburg, Pennsylvania, for impersonating a soldier. Before her arrest, Ida had seen action at South Mountain and Antietam. She also had been with the 11th New York at Gettysburg. She was released from prison in 1864. Later on, her sex was discovered again, when she was arrested for public drunkenness.

## ROSE ROONEY

Mrs. Rose Rooney of New Orleans served four years with the 15th Louisiana Infantry. She marched with them and rallied the troops in battle. Rose served as mother, confidant, and cook for the 15th Louisiana until she was mustered out at war's end.

## ANNIE SAHALSKI

Annie Blanche Sahalski, an army widow, was an excellent marksman as well as equestrian. She often led troops into battle after the officers had fallen. Annie wore clothing she had made of wolf skins. Everywhere Annie went, she was attended by thirteen very large dogs. When General Sherman encountered her he shouted, "What the devil of a creature is that? Wild woman, Pawnee, Sioux, or what?"

## MARY SCARBERRY

Mary Scarberry (also shown as Seaberry) from Columbus, Ohio, assumed the persona of Charles Freemen to fight in the Civil War so slavery would be ended. When Mary was hospitalized with a fever, probably typhoid, her gender was revealed. Mary was expelled from Company F, 52nd Ohio Regiment for being sexually incompatible with the unit on November 10, 1862.

## Otto Schaffer

A farmer from Butler County, Kansas, named Otto Schaffer served four years in a Kansas regiment. He was discovered to be a woman only when the body was prepared for burial after Otto was killed in a skirmish.

## Mary Seizgle

A Northern soldier's diary recorded Mary Seizgle's arrest for impersonating a soldier in the 41st New York Infantry. She, like Ida Remington, spent the remainder of the war in prison.

## Mary Smith

Mary Smith enlisted in McClellan Zouaves, 41st Ohio Infantry, to avenge her only brother's untimely death at Bull Run. She was discovered at Camp Wood when she wrung out a dish towel instead of shaking it as her male counterparts would have.

## Susie King Taylor

Susie King Taylor, a black woman and former slave, served in the 1st South Carolina Regiment, a Union unit. She enlisted with her husband, brothers, and several other relatives and served for four years. "I could shoot straight, and often hit the target," Susie bragged. She knew how to dismantle, clean, and reassemble her weapon. Susie also performed nursing and cleaning duties. For her distinguished acts of heroism, she received no compensation.

## Ellen P. L. Thompson

Ellen P. L. Thompson was mustered into the 139th Illinois Infantry. No further accounts are recorded.

## Tommy

Tommy, an Anglo-African, enlisted at Lancaster, Kentucky into the 12th Rhode Island Infantry. He served as a bodyguard for one of the captains and saw action on several fronts. When he mustered out with the regiment, it was revealed that Tommy was actually a twenty year old woman.

## NANCY SLAUGHTER WALKER

Nancy Slaughter Walker dressed in men's clothing and became a rough rider with William Quantrill's troopers. She continued to ride with the raiders after the war, becoming one of their notorious outlaw band.

## CHARLES H. WILLIAMS

A female known only as Charles H. Williams served in the Second Iowa Infantry. She enlisted to be near her lover, like so many other women did.

## JOANNA WILLIAMS

Company M, 17th Missouri Infantry had a soldier named John Williams who happened to be Miss JoAnna Williams.

## LAURA J. WILLIAMS

Laura J. Williams of Arkansas assumed the persona of Lieutenant Henry Benford and led a troops of Texans at Shiloh. She served in several other campaigns but history does not reveal which ones.

## MAGGIE WILSON

Maggie Wilson, also known as Charles Marshall, a private in the 13th New York Regulars, was discovered early in the war. Not wishing to return home, Maggie chose to remain with the 13th as a vivandiere.

## MARY WISE

Mary Wise served two years in the 34th Indiana Volunteers before being mustered out. According to the *New York Herald*, dated August 14, 1864, Mary was wounded five times.

## MARY WRIGHT

Mary Wright and Mary Henry were Southern ladies who were arrested in uniform two weeks before General Robert E. Lee's surrender at Appomatox. The "dashing young creatures" were captured by Union soldiers and imprisoned in Nashville, Tennessee.

# NOTES

## Introduction

1. Mary Ashton Livermore, *My Story Of The War* (Hartford, CT: A. D. Worthington & Co., 1887), 16.
2. Bell I. Wiley, *The Life Of Billy Yank* (New Orleans, LA: Louisiana State University Press, 1952), 337.
3. David S. Sparks, *Inside Lincoln's Army*, 130.
4. S. B. Anthony, *History Of Women's Suffrage*, 1889, 36.
5. *New Albany, (Indiana) Ledger*, July 9, 1862.
6. *Cincinnati (Ohio) Dollar Times*, August 11, 1864.
7. S. B. Anthony, *The History Of Women's Suffrage*, 1880, 36.
8. *Maysville (Kentucky) Dollar Weekly Bulletin*, November 27, 1862.

## Nancy Harts

Clark Johnson, "The Nancy Harts Were Gallant Ladies," *LaGrange (Georgia) Daily News*, December 17, 1936.

"LaGrange Sent Nancy Harts to Battle During the War of '64," *LaGrange (Georgia) Daily News*, January 19, 1937.

"Early History of Old Washington," *Dayton (Ohio) Herald*, December 18, 1915.

## Rhea County Girls

V. C. Allen, *Rhea And Meigs Counties In The Confederate War* (Haywood, TN: Higginson Book & Co., 1976).

Bette J. Broyles, *History Of Rhea County, Tennessee* (Nashville, TN: Tennessee Historical Society, 1976.

"Rhea County's Girl Warriors," *Chattanooga (Tennessee) Sunday Times*, March 6, 1938.

## Bess Dell & Company

Catherine Cooper Hopley, *Life In The South, 1863,* (Chapel Hill, NC: University of North Carolina Press), 60-61.

George C. Rable, *Civil Wars,* (Chicago: University of Illinois Press, 1989), 152.

"The Journal of Bettie Rid by Blackmore," *Tennessee Historical Quarterly*, March, 1953.

## Fauquier County, Virginia Women

*The War Of Rebellion: A Compilation Of The Official Records Of The Union And Confederate Armies.* 128 vols. in 4 series. (Washington, D. C.: U. S. Government Printing Office 1880-1901), 247.

## Charlotte Anderson

Richard Hall, *Patriots In Disguise,* (Marlowe and Co., 1993), 197, 203.

## Mrs. John Bakr

R. M. Devens, *Pictorial Book of Anecdotes of The Rebellion* (St. Louis, MO: J. H. Mason, 1889) 122.

## Arabella Barlow

L. P. Brockett and Mary C. Vaughn, *Woman's Work In The Civil War* (Philadelphia: Zeigler McCurdy & Co., 1867), 225-233.

Brigadier General John B. Gordon, *Reminiscences Of Civil War* (New York: Charles Scribner's Sons, 1889), 105.

## Mollie Bean

*Woman's Work In The Civil War*, 303.

*Richmond (Virginia) Examiner*, October 31, 1864 and November 25, 1864.

*Sandusky (Virginia) Record*, December 12, 1864.

**Mary and Mollie Bell**
Mary Elizabeth Massey, *Bonnet Brigades* (New York: Alfred A. Knopf, 1867) 84-85.

**Malinda Blaylock**
Walter Clark, *Histories Of The Several Regiments And Battalions From North Carolina In The Great War* (Raleigh, NC: State of North Carolina Press, 1901) 330-331.
*Fayetteville (North Carolina) Observer*, October 2, 1923.
William F. Fox, *Regimental Losses In The American Civil War* (Dayton, OH: Morningside Books, reprint of 1889 original), 60.

**Madame Boivert**
Frank Moore, *Women of the War* (Hartford, CT: S. S. Scranton & Co., 1886) 30.

**Harriett Brown**
Richard Hall, *Patriots In Disguise* (New York: Marlowe & Co., 1993), 197.

**Kady Brownell**
*Woman's Work In The Civil War*, 747-753.
*Frank Leslie's Illustrated Newspaper*, August 17, 1862.
Ethel Alice Hurn, *Wisconsin Women In The War* (Madison, WI: Wisconsin Historical Commission, 1865), 110.
*Women of the War*, 54-64.

**Florena Budwin**
Stewart Sikasis, *Who Was Who in the Civil War* (New York: Facts On File Publishing Co., 1986) 86.
Veterans Administration Records, January 25, 1865, Fort Gibson National Cemetery, Oklahoma.

**Mary Burns**
*Detroit (Michigan) Advertiser And Tribune*, February 25, 1863.
*Wisconsin Women In The War*, 103.
*Frank Leslie's Illustrated Newspaper*, December 19, 1863.

*New York Herald*, December 28, 1863 and January 7, 1864.

**Canadian Lou**
*Memphis (Tennessee) Bulletin*, December 18, 1862.

**Captain Billy**
Frank Moore, *The Rebellion 1861-1865* (Madison, WI: S. S. Scranton & Co., 1887) 44.

**Frances Clalin**
William C. Davis, *The Common Soldier of the Civil War* (New York: Random House, 1962), 34.
Albert A. Nofi, *Civil Wars* (New York: DeCapo Publishing, 1956), 357.

**Amy Clarke**
*Augusta (Georgia) Chronicle And Sentinel*, January 8, 1863.
*Cairo City (Georgia) Gazette*, December 25, 1863.
Henry W. R. Jackson, *Southern Women Of The Second American Revolution* (Atlanta, GA: 1863), 7.
*Jackson Mississippian*, December 30, 1862.

**Frances Louisa Clayton**
*Cincinnati (Ohio) Gazette*, October 2, 1863.
*Frank Leslie's Illustrated Newspaper*, December 19, 1863.
*Grand Rapids (Michigan) Eagle*, November 12, 1863.
*Wellsburg (West Virginia) Herald*, October 19, 1863.

**Sarah Collins**
*Frank Leslie's Illusatrated Newspaper*, December 19, 1863.
*Wisconsin Women In The War*, 103-106.
*New York Herald*, December 28, 1863.

**Elizabeth Compton**
John Hiesley, "Ladies in our Wars," *Antique Week*, May 29, 1989.
*Frank Leslie's Illustrated Newspaper*, December 19, 1863.
Alfred Guernsey and Henry Allen, *Harper's Pictorial History of the Civil*

*War* (New York: Harper & Brothers, 1866-1868), 532.

Frazar Kirkland, *Pictorial Book of Ancedotes of the Rebellion* (St. Louis, MO: J. H. Mason Publisher, 1889), 204.

*New York Herald*, December 28, 1863.

### Lizzie Cook
*Pictorial Book of Anecdotes of the Rebellion*, 204.

### Mary Corbin
Colonel Caleb Carlton's Papers, 89th Ohio, Massachusetts Division, Library of Congress, August 27, 1863 and September 15, 1863.

### Lucy Cox
Mrs. John H. Logan, *The Part Taken by Women in American History* (Wil-mington, DE: Perry-Nolle Publishing, 1912), 492.

### Sophia Cryer
Records of the 11th Pennsylvania, Company A, National Archives and Records Administration, Washington, D. C.

### Mrs. Curtis
*Richmond (Virginia) Whig*, January 23, 1862.

Agatha Young, *The Women And The Crisis* (Oblensky, NY: McDowell Publishing, 1959), 123.

### Amelia Davis
*O.R.*, 247.

### Catherine E. Davidson
*Civil War*, 357.

### Frances Day
Ted Alexander, *The 126th Pennsylvania* (Chicago: Beers & Co, 184).

Fox, William F., *Regimental Losses in the Civil War* (Albany, NY: Albany Publishing) 60.

Roster for Company C, 126th Pennsylvania Infantry, NARA, Washington, D.C.

### Mrs. L. L. Deming
Records for 10th Michigan Infantry, NARA, Washington, D. C.

### Mary Dennis
John Laffin, *Women In Battle* (London: Brassey Publishing, 1967), 52.

### Bridget Divers
*Woman's Work In The Civil War*, 770-774.

*Frank Leslie's Illustrated Newspaper*, August 17, 1862.

*Wisconsin Women In The War*, 100-102.

*My Story Of The War*, 116-119.

*Women Of The War*, 109-112.

*Life Of Billy Yank*, 339.

### Dutch Mary
John Haley, December 29, 1862, journal entry, NARA, 64.

Ruth L. Silliker, *The Rebel Yell And The Yankee Hurrah* (Camden, ME: Down East Books, 1985).

### Sarah Edmonds
Sarah Emma Edmonds, *Nurse And Spy* (W. S. Williams & Co., 1864).

*Fort Scott (Kansas) Weekly Monitor*, January 17, 1884.

William F. Fox, *Regimental Losses In The American Civil War* (Albany, NY: Albany Publishing, 1889), 60.

House Reports #820 and 849, NARA.

*Kansas City (Kansas) Times*, March 1884.

*Lansing (Michigan) State Republican*, June 20, 21, and 26, 1900.

General John Robertson, *Michigan In The War* (Durham, SC: Education Co., 1882), 36-37.

### Mrs. Ellis
*Pictorial Book of Anecdotes of the Rebellion*, 114.

### Emily
Rossiter Johnson, *Campfire And Battlefield* (New York: Civil War Press, 1967), 30.

*Women Of The War*, 529.

## Anna Etheridge
*Woman's Work In The Civil War*, 749-53.
*Frank Leslie's Illustrated Newspaper*, August 17, 1862.
*My Life In The War*, 118-119.

## Hannah Ewbank
*Wisconsin Women In The War*, 100.

## Amanda Fanham
Agatha Young, *The Women And The Crisis* (Oblensky, NY: McDowell, 1959),100.

## Elizabeth Cain Finnan
*National Tribune*, July 25, 1907.
United States Army Military History Institute, Records 2984, Carlisle, Pennsylvania.

## Augusta Foster
*The Women And The Crisis*, 125.

## Frank
*The Rebellion 1861-1865*, 44.

## Mary Galloway
"An Army Surgeon's Story," *St. Louis, Illinois Magazine*, April 1883, 137-150.

## Ella Hobart Gibson
*Reminiscences Of The Civil War*, 31-41.
*New York Herald*, January 18, 1965.
OP Pension File #W3370, NARA.

## Ellen Goodridge
*Brooklyn Daily Times*, February 20, 1864.
*Women Of The War*, 532-533.

## Nellie Graves
*Frank Leslie's Illustrated Newspaper*, March 7, 1863.
*New York Herald*, December 18, 1863.
*New York Sun*, February 10, 1901.

## Elsa Guerin
Gertrude Asherton, *Can Women Be Gentlemen?* (Boston, MA: Wallace and Spooner, 1938).
Fred M. Mazzulla and William Jostka, *Mountain Charley Or The Adven-*

*tures Of Mrs. E. J. Guerin Who Was Thirteen Years In Male Attire* (Norman, OK: University of Oklahoma Press, 1968).

## Edward O. Hamilton
*The Rebellion 1861-1865*, 96.

## Mary Hancock
John Laffin, *Women In Battle* (London: Brassey Publishing, 1967), 51.

## Charles Hatfield
United States Army Military History Institute, Reference 57, Carlisle, Pennsylvania.

## Margaret Henry
*The Mississippian*, December 31, 1862.
*Washington Chronicle*, March 30, 1865.

## Bridget Higgins
*O.R.*, 227.

## Mary Hill
Ella Lonn, *Foreigners In The Confederacy* (Boston, MA: Peter Smith, 1965).

## Jane Hinsdale
*Women Of The War*, 109-112.

## Irene Hodgers
Linus P. Brockett, *The Camp, The Battlefield, And The Hospital* (Hartford, CT: L. Stebbins, 1869), 70-72.
J. T. Headley, THE GREAT REBELLION (New York: Neal Publishing, 1866), 167-169.
Illinois Veterans Home Administration Papers, December 12, 1915.
*O.R.*; Pension File, November 12, 1913.
*Pittsburg (Illinois) Republican*, May 14, 1913.
*Quincy (Illinois) Whig*, May 5, 1913.
Veterans Administration Records, Pension File #1,001, NARA, 132.
*Washington Sunday Star*, March 29, 1913.

## Mary Hollingsworth
*Wisconsin Women Of The War*, 109.

**Frances Hook**
*National Tribune,* August 29, 1895.
*New York Sun,* February 10, 1901.
*Michigan In The War,* 95-101.
United States Army Military History Institute, Reference Number 1674, Carlisle, Pennsylvania.

**Lucinda Horne**
*Chapman's History Of Edgefield County* (New York: Castle Books, 1891), 483491.
C. Kay Larson, "Bonny Yank and Ginny Reb," *Minerva,* (Pasadena, MD: Minerva Press, Spring 1990), 33-48.

**Kate Howe**
*National Tribune,* September 10, 1885 and October 26, 1885, October 29, 1885, and December 10, 1885.
USAMHI, Number 4729, Carlisle, PA.

**Satronia Hunt**
Thomas P. Lowry, *The Story The Soldiers Wouldn't Tell* (Fredericksburg, VA: Sgt. Kirkland's Museum, 1994), 121.

**Elvira Ibecker**
*Campfire And Battlefield,* 18.
Records for Company F, 126th Pennsylvania, NARA, Washington, D.C.

**Mary Jane Jackson**
Journal Entry of W. W. Sprague, 13th Massachusetts, Company B, Belle Island Prison, December 19, 1863.
USAMHI, Reference Number 652.

**Mary Jenkins**
*The Story Soldiers Wouldn't Tell,* 121.

**Charles Johehous**
Pension File #1,070,204, Veterans Administration Records, NARA.
*National Tribune,* May 13, 1886.

**Annie E. Jones**
Adjutant General's Papers, Record Group 19, NARA.
*New York Herald,* September 16, 1863.

**Lizzie Jones**
*Pictorial Book of Anecdotes of the Rebellion.*

**Mrs. Albee Kamoo**
*Lancaster (Pennsylvania) Herald,* 1904.

**Kate**
Henry C. Bear, *Civil War Letters* (Chattanooga, TN: Lincoln Memorial University Press, 1961).
*Historical Register and Dictionary of the United States Army,* Vol. II, 1903.

**Annie Lillibridge**
*The Pictorial Book Of Ancedotes Of The Rebellion,* 621.
Captain John Truesdale, *The Bluecoats* (Boston, MA: Jones Brothers, 1867), 54.

**Mademoiselle Major**
Captain D. P. Coyningham, *Sherman's March Through The South,* 194-197.
Fitzgerald Ross, *A Visit To The Cities And Camps Of The Confederate States* (Edinborough: Blackwood & Sons, 1863), 97-101.
*Lynchburg (Virginia) Virginian,* October 6, 1864.
Frances Simplins and James W. Tatton, *Women Of The Confederacy* (Richmond, VA: Garrett & Massie, 1936), 80-81.

**Barbara Malpass**
*O. R.,* Records #27, NARA.

**Julie Marcum**
Ida Tarbell's Letter, NARA.

**Charles Martin**
Lee Middleton, *Hearts Of Fire* (Franklin, NC: Genealogy Publishing Service, 1993), 97.

**Mary McCreary**
Records of 21st Ohio, Company H, NARA.

**Marion McKenzie**
"Harry Fitzallen," *Wheeling (Ohio) Intelligencer,* December 25, 1862,

and January 9, 1863.

**Charlie Miler**
Records of 18th New York Infantry, NARA.

**Madeline Moore**
Madeline Moore, *The Lady Lieutenant: The Strange And Thrilling Adventures Of Miss Madeline Moore* (Boston, MA: Walker Wise, 1867).
David Truby, *Women At War* (New York: Paladin Press,1977), 27.

**LaBelle Morgan**
*Women In Battle*, 51.

**Sue Mundy**
*Pictorial Book Of Anecdotes Of The Rebellion*, 287-296.

**Mary Murphy**
Records of Company B, 53rd Massachusetts Infantry, NARA.

**Nellie A. K.**
Ferdinado Sarmiento, *Life Of Pauline Cushman* (Philadelphia: John C. Potter & Co., 1865), 368-370.

**Elizabeth Niles**
DeAnne Blanton, "Women Soldiers of the Civil War," *National Archives Quarterly*, Spring, 1993.

**Mary Owens**
*Frank Leslie's Illustrated Newspaper*, March 7, 1863.
*Women Of The War*, 529-533.
*New York Herald*, October 14, 1861.

**Aramita Palmer**
*O.R.*, 229.

**Rebecca Parish**
*O. R.*, 247.

**Bell Patterson**
*New York Herald*, May 1, 1886.

**Melvina Peppercorn**
Wayne R. Austerman, Meriwether's "Recollection of Ninety-Two Years, 18241916," "Lock and Load, Miss Scarlett," *Southern Partisan*, Fall 1998.

*The Women And The Crisis*, 95.

**Mary Perkins**
*Women Of The War*, 30.

**Georgianna Peterman**
*My Story Of The War*, 119.

**Belle Peterson**
*Wisconsin Women In The War*, 100-103.

**Bettie Taylor Phillips**
Matthew Andrews, *Women Of The South In War Times* (Baltimore, OH: Norman Remington, 1920), 120-126.

**Mary Ann Pittman**
Wayne R. Austerman, "Lock and Load, Miss Scarlett."

**Harriett Redd**
*O. R.*, 247-248.

**Georgia T. Reed**
*Wisconsin Women Of The War*, 109.

**Ida Remington**
*Detroit Advertiser And Tribune*, August 27, 1863.

**Ella Reno**
Daniel Reed Larned Papers, Library of Congress, May 14 and 15, 1864.

**Belle Reynolds**
*Women Of The War*, 254-277.
*The Women And The Crisis*.

**Rose Rooney**
Mary Logan, *The Part Taken by Women in American History* (Wilmington, DE: Perry-Nolle Publishing, 1912), 492-93.

**Annie Shalaski**
Rosalind Miles, *The Women's History Of The World* (Tapfield, MA: Salem House, 1988), 171.

**Otto Schaffer**
Record Group 94, NARA.

**Mary Scarberry**
Regimental Records of Company F, 52nd Illinois Infantry, NARA.

**Mary Seizgle**
*The Rebellion*, 48.

**Mary Smith**
*Cleveland (Ohio) Plain Dealer*, September 10, 1861.

**Bettie Sullivan**
*Women Of The South In War Times*, 112-115.

**Sarah Taylor**
*Pictorial Book Of Anecodotes Of The Rebellion*, 59.
*Frank Leslie's Heroic Incidents*, 4-6

**Susie Taylor King**
Susie Taylor King, *Reminiscences Of My Life In Camp* (New York: Arno Publishing, 1902).

**Marie Tepe**
*Pictorial Book Of Anecdotes Of The Rebellion*, 63.
*Historical Times Illustrated Encyclopedia* (New York: Harper & Row, 1986), 744745.
Frank Rauscha, *Music Of The March 1862-1865* (Philadelphia: William F. Fell & Co, 1892), 68.

**Ellen Thompson**
Records of the 139th Illinois Infantry, NARA.

**Lucy Thompson**
Joseph H. Crute, *Units Of The Confederate States Army* (Midlothian, VA: Derwent Books, 1987).
Regimental Records of the 18th North Carolina Infantry, NARA.

**Tommy**
*Pictorial Book Of Anecdotes Of The Rebellion*, 193.

**Madame Turchin**
*Anderson's Story Of The Illinois Central Lines During The Civil War* (Cairo, IL: Illinois State Historical Society).
*Woman's Work In The Civil War*, 770-771.
*New York Herald*, August 4, 1862.

**Loreta Velasquez**
*Women Of The War-Times*, 112-115.
John Headley, *The Great Rebellion* (New York: Neale Publishing,1866), 262-274.
John Headley, *Confederate Operations In Canada And New York* (New York: Neale Publishing, 1906), 376-380.
*Louisville (Kentucky) Daily Journal*, October 9, 1861.
*Lynchburg (Tennessee) Daily Journal*, July 4, 1867.
*New Orleans Picayune*, January 5, 1867.
James Parton, *General Butler In New Orleans* (New York: Mason Brothers, 1864), 311.
*Richmond Daily Examiner*, July 2, 1863.
*Richmond Daily Whig*, June 19, 1863.
Loreta Janeta Velasquez, *The Woman In Battle, A Narrative Of The Exploits, Adventures, And Travels Of Madame Loreta Janeta Velasquez Otherwise Known As Lieutenant Harry T. Buford, Confederate States Army* (Hartford, CT. T. Balknap, 1874).

**Sarah Wakeman**
Lauren Cook Burgess, *An Uncommon Soldier* (Pasadena, MD: Minerva Center, 1994).

**Nancy Walker**
Walter P. Lane, *The Adventures And Recollections Of Walter P. Lane, 1887*, NARA, 93-95.

**Charles Williams**
Regimental Records, 2nd Iowa Infantry, NARA.

**JoAnna Williams**
*O.R.*, Records of Company M, 17th Missouri Infantry, NARA.

**Laura Williams**
*Civil War*, 359.

### Eliza Wilson
*Wisconsin Women Of The War*, 108.
Marine United States Army General Hospital Records #6747, New Orleans, LA.

### Fannie Wilson
John W. Heisly, "Ladies in Our Wars," *Antique Week*, May 29, 1989, 12.
*Frank Leslie's Illustrated Newspaper*, Mary 7, 1863.
*New York Herald*, December 18, 1863.
*New York Sun*, February 10, 1901.

### Maggie Wilson
Catherine Clinton, *The Other Civil War* (New York: Hill & Wong, 1984), 85.

### Mary Wise
*Bonnet Brigades*, 84-86.
*New York Herald*, August 12 and 14, 1864.

### Mary Wright
*The Southern Women Of The Second American Revolution*, 9.
*The Mississippian*, December 30, 1862.
*Washington Chronicle*, March 30, 1865.

## *ABOUT THE AUTHOR*

Dr. Rebecca D. Early Larson, a graduate of University of Mary Hardin-Baylor, California State, and Honolulu University, teaches social studies at Temple High School in Temple, Texas. A descendant of the Confederate General Jubal Early, a fact which sparked her intense interest in the Civil War, Rebecca has found herself drawn to the stories of women who served in the conflict whether behind the lines as spies and nurses or in the heat of battle.

Her hobbies include raising miniature and toy dachshunds and registered miniature and quarter horses, scuba diving, and historical outings. She and her husband of thirty years live in Troy, Texas, and have one daughter.

THOMAS PUBLICATIONS publishes books about the American Colonial era, the Revolutionary War, the Civil War, and other important topics. For a complete list of titles, please visit our web site:

http://thomaspublications.com

Or write to:

THOMAS PUBLICATIONS
P.O. Box 3031
Gettysburg, PA 17325